SINGING IN THE
REIGN

THE PSALMS AND THE
LITURGY OF GOD'S KINGDOM

EMMAUS
ROAD
PUBLISHING

Michael Barber
Introduction by Scott Hahn

*To my parents,
who have taught me
the most valuable lessons
in life-giving love*

SINGING IN THE REIGN

THE PSALMS AND THE LITURGY OF GOD'S KINGDOM

EMMAUS
ROAD
PUBLISHING

Michael Barber
Introduction by Scott Hahn

Nihil Obstat
Rev. James Dunfee
Censor Librorum

Imprimatur ✠
Most Rev. Gilbert I. Sheldon, D.D., D.Min.

© 2001
Emmaus Road Publishing
All rights reserved.

Library of Congress catalog no. 2001093409

Published by
Emmaus Road Publishing
a division of Catholics United for the Faith
827 North Fourth Street
Steubenville, Ohio 43952
(800) 398-5470

Cover design and layout by
Beth Hart

The cover artwork is *The Triumph of David*
by Matteo Rosselli, located in the Louvre, Paris, France.
Used with permission of Réunion des Musées Nationaux /
Art Resource, New York.

Published in the United States of America
ISBN 1-931018-08-1

CONTENTS

Abbreviations 7

Introduction by Scott Hahn, Ph.D. 11

Chapter 1
Psalm Background to Studying the Psalter 31

—PART I: A Theology of the Psalter—
Chapter 2
The Davidic Covenant as Old Testament Climax 39

Chapter 3
Themes of the Psalter 59

Chapter 4
A Canonical Study of the Book of Psalms 81
    Book I (1-41) 86
    Book II (42-72) 92
    Book III (73-89) 105
    Book IV (90-106) 118
    Book V (107-50) 126

—PART II: Jesus and the Restoration of the Kingdom—
Chapter 5
Restoring All Things in Christ 137

Chapter 6
Jesus and the Restoration of the Kingdom 143

Chapter 7
The Church: The Kingdom of God on Earth 149

Epilogue
Romans 9-11:
God's Fatherly Plan for Finding the Lost Tribes 155

The Structure of the Book of Psalms 175

Recommended Reading 177

Bibliography 179

ABBREVIATIONS

The Old Testament

Gen./Genesis
Ex./Exodus
Lev./Leviticus
Num./Numbers
Deut./Deuteronomy
Josh./Joshua
Judg./Judges
Ruth/Ruth
1 Sam./1 Samuel
2 Sam./2 Samuel
1 Kings/1 Kings
2 Kings/2 Kings
1 Chron./1 Chronicles
2 Chron./2 Chronicles
Ezra/Ezra
Neh./Nehemiah
Tob./Tobit
Jud./Judith
Esther/Esther
Job/Job
Ps./Psalms
Prov./Proverbs
Eccles./Ecclesiastes
Song/Song of Solomon
Wis./Wisdom
Sir./Sirach (Ecclesiasticus)
Is./Isaiah
Jer./Jeremiah
Lam./Lamentations
Bar./Baruch
Ezek./Ezekiel
Dan./Daniel
Hos./Hosea

Joel/Joel
Amos/Amos
Obad./Obadiah
Jon./Jonah
Mic./Micah
Nahum/Nahum
Hab./Habakkuk
Zeph./Zephaniah
Hag./Haggai
Zech./Zechariah
Mal./Malachi
1 Mac./1 Maccabees
2 Mac./2 Maccabees

The New Testament

Mt./Matthew
Mk./Mark
Lk./Luke
Jn./John
Acts/Acts of the Apostles
Rom./Romans
1 Cor./1 Corinthians
2 Cor./2 Corinthians
Gal./Galatians
Eph./Ephesians
Phil./Philippians
Col./Colossians
1 Thess./1 Thessalonians
2 Thess./2 Thessalonians
1 Tim./1 Timothy
2 Tim./2 Timothy
Tit./Titus
Philem./Philemon
Heb./Hebrews

Jas./James
1 Pet./1 Peter
2 Pet./2 Peter
1 Jn./1 John
2 Jn./2 John
3 Jn./3 John
Jude/Jude
Rev./Revelation (Apocalypse)

Documents of Vatican II

SC   Constitution on the Sacred Liturgy
(*Sacrosanctum Concilium*), December 4, 1963

IM   Decree on the Means of Social Communication
(*Inter Mirifica*), December 4, 1963

LG   Dogmatic Constitution on the Church
(*Lumen Gentium*), November 21, 1964

OE   Decree on the Catholic Eastern Churches
(*Orientalium Ecclesiarum*), November 21, 1964

UR   Decree on Ecumenism
(*Unitatis Redintegratio*), November 21, 1964

CD   Decree on the Pastoral Office of Bishops in the Church
(*Christus Dominus*), October 28, 1965

PC   Decree on the Up-to-Date Renewal of Religious Life
(*Perfectae Caritatis*), October 28, 1965

OT   Decree on the Training of Priests
(*Optatam Totius*), October 28, 1965

GE   Declaration on Christian Education
(*Gravissimum Educationis*), October 28, 1965

NA   Declaration on the Relation of the Church to
Non-Christian Religions (*Nostra Aetate*), October 28, 1965

DV   Dogmatic Constitution on Divine Revelation
(*Dei Verbum*), November 18, 1965

AA   Decree on the Apostolate of Lay People
(*Apostolicam Actuositatem*), November 18, 1965

DH   Declaration on Religious Liberty
(*Dignitatis Humanae*), December 7, 1965

AG   Decree on the Church's Missionary Activity
(*Ad Gentes Divinitus*), December 7, 1965

PO   Decree on the Ministry and Life of Priests
(*Presbyterorum Ordinis*), December 7, 1965

GS   Pastoral Constitution on the Church in the
Modern World (*Gaudium et Spes*), December 7, 1965

*All quotations from the documents of the Second Vatican Council are taken from Austin Flannery, O.P., ed., *Vatican II: The Conciliar and Post Conciliar Documents*, Northport, NY: Costello Publishing Co., copyright © 1975.

Catechism of the Catholic Church

Throughout the text, the *Catechism of the Catholic Church* (United States Catholic Conference—Libreria Editrice Vaticana, 1994, as revised in the 1997 Latin typical edition) will be cited simply as "Catechism."

INTRODUCTION

Shaking Out the Psalter

No portion of Scripture is so familiar to Catholics as the Psalms. It is the only book of the Bible that is read at every Mass, and the responsorial psalm is the only Scripture reading of the Mass that the congregation recites along with the lector, cantor, or priest. It's likely, too, that on any given Sunday, any given Catholic will sing a hymn adapted from the Psalms. From "O God, Our Help in Ages Past" and "Bringing in the Sheaves" to "Sing a New Song" and "On Eagles' Wings"—the Psalms rank among the most-sung items in any hymnal.

It's no wonder, then, that the lines of these ancient Hebrew poems come so readily to our minds and our lips.

"The Lord is my shepherd, I shall not want" (23:1).
"O taste and see that the Lord is good!" (34:8).
"Out of the mouths of babes . . ." (8:2).
"Keep me as the apple of Your eye" (17:8).
"The Lord is my light and my salvation" (27:1).
"Deep calls to deep" (42:7).
"Make a joyful noise to the Lord" (98:7).
"Teach us to number our days" (90:12).

Worship Is a Psalm Occasion

The list could run on for pages. And this is hardly a modern phenomenon. For all of Christian history, the Psalms have provided the most quoted and quotable passages of Scripture. The Psalter is, by far, the Old Testament book quoted most frequently in the New Testament. It is the Old Testament book most contemplated by the Fathers of the Church. From the earliest times, the Psalms have filled the days of monks and nuns. In the ancient Church, there were monasteries given to perpetual recitation of the Psalms—round the clock, all year long. To this day, cloistered communities still recite all 150 psalms. In the West, they do so in the course of each week; in the East, every two weeks.

So no one could credibly claim that the Psalms have been ignored in the life of the Church. Nor will I. But I do believe that the Psalms have been underappreciated, even where they've been most diligently read or chanted. The problem—and it's a good problem to have—comes from our delight in each individual psalm. For each and every one is a unique poetic gem. Each psalm gleams with its own insight, its own manner of expression. Each psalm can stand on its own literary merits.

Yet I maintain, with a growing number of scholars, that we can't fully appreciate these gems unless we see them in their intended setting—a setting intended by their human anthologists and by their divine Author. We need to see the structural unity of the entire Psalter (in its final, canonical form), the narrative thread that runs from Psalm 1 to 150.

Verse-Case Scenario

What is the Psalter? What is a psalm? These words appear odd to readers of English, and they would appear just as strange to the ancient Hebrews who wrote the Psalms. Both "psalm" and "Psalter" are English renderings of the words applied to the poems in the Greek translation of the Old Testament. *Psalterion* is Greek for a stringed instrument, a sort of harp; a *psalmos* is a song sung to the accompaniment of strings.

The Israelites, however, called these lyrics *Tehillim*, or praises. The earliest Hebrew witnesses to the Psalter called it *Sefer Tehillim*, the Book of Praises.

It's clear, from the texts themselves, that the Psalms were meant to be sung or chanted in a formal, cultic setting.

Some include instructions (for example, "To the choirmaster"); others specify the musical instruments to be used in accompaniment. Many of the psalms were integral to the liturgical worship of the Jerusalem Temple. Indeed, the Psalter has often been called the "Hymnal of the Second Temple," for the book probably reached its final form at that time—that is, in the post-exilic period.

The first Temple, built by Solomon, the son of David, in the tenth century B.C., had been destroyed by the Babylonian invaders in 587 B.C. (cf. 2 Kings 24-25). In 539 B.C., however, a decree of King Cyrus of Persia permitted the people of Judea to return to the land and rebuild the Temple. This structure, much diminished from Solomon's original, was called the second Temple; it would be renovated and expanded on a grand scale during the reign of the Herods (first century A.D.). Thus the period of the second Temple stretched from 515 B.C. until the utter destruction of Jerusalem by the Romans in 70 A.D.

The Temple was the natural habitat of most of the psalms. The rabbis record in the *Mishnah* that each day the Levites sang certain appointed psalms: Psalm 24 on Sunday; 48 on Monday; 82 on Tuesday; 94 on Wednesday; 81 on Thursday; 93 on Friday; and 92 on Saturday, the Sabbath. Other psalms accompanied the liturgies and sacrifices that renewed the covenant God had made with Israel, with Moses, and with the house of David. Some scholars hold that as many as half of the psalms were integral to the Temple liturgies. Others were associated with the liturgies of the synagogue, where they were probably read rather than sung. Still others found their place in the liturgies of the home, such as the Passover Seder meal, which culminated in the recitation of the hallel psalms (113-18 and 135).

Fit from a King

Most of what we know about the liturgical use of the Psalms, we know from the period of the second Temple. Yet many of the Psalms surely predate that period. The Psalter attributes around half the psalms to King David (84 in the Septuagint, the ancient Greek translation; 73 in the medieval Masoretic text). Others are credited to Moses, Solomon, Asaph, Heman, Ethan, and the Sons of Korah. Some of these people appear in the Old Testament narratives as renowned performers of sacred music (cf. 1 Chron. 15:16-22; Neh. 12:41-46).

David, however, remains the psalmist *par excellence*, even though he did not live to see the first Temple built. He is known as "the sweet psalmist of Israel" (2 Sam. 23:1). Jesus acknowledges David's authorship of Psalm 110 (cf. Mt. 22:41-45), while Paul calls David the author of Psalms 32 and 69 (cf. Rom. 4:6-8, 11:9-10). The Letter to the Hebrews identifies David as the author of Psalm 95 (Heb. 4:7).

Thus many of the psalms were composed even before the time of Solomon's Temple—and not only those that bear David's byline, but also those attributed to contemporaries of David, such as Asaph. Still other psalms, such as 72 and 127, claim Solomon as their author, and so trace their origins to the first Temple.

One thing is certain: The Psalter is permeated with a Davidic spirituality. Its prayers reflect the particular terms of the covenant God made with the house of David. And we must not underestimate the significance of God's covenant with David or its difference from the covenant with Moses. The Mosaic covenant, made on Sinai, was a national and exclusive covenant with Israel. The Davidic covenant, made on Zion, was international and was inclusive of both Israelites and Gentiles. Israel's worship in the desert had been a relatively simple affair; but, for the Temple, David had to orchestrate a whole new form of covenantal worship, befitting a united family of Israelites and Gentiles.

In fact, the Psalter emphasizes what is distinctive about the covenant with David and what sets it apart from God's earlier covenant with Moses. According to Saint Hippolytus:

> The book of Psalms contains new doctrine after the law of Moses. And after the writing of Moses, it is the second book of doctrine. Now, after the death of Moses and Joshua, and after the judges, arose David, who . . . first gave to the Hebrews a new style of psalmody, by which he abrogates the ordinances established by Moses with respect to sacrifices, and introduces the new hymn and a new style of jubilant praise in the worship of God; and throughout his whole ministry he teaches very many other things that went beyond the law of Moses.

Throughout the Psalms we find a more universal message; for to David God had given kingship not only over Israel, but over "the nations"—the Gentiles—as well. Throughout the Psalms we find a deep piety for the Temple, the house that David had pledged to raise up for Yahweh. We find reverence for Jerusalem, David's capital city, and for the king who rules, in God's name, over a united Israel. Indeed, we see the attribution of a priestly character to the king of Israel (cf. Ps. 110:4).

Getting It Together

Nevertheless, it is accurate to call the Psalter the "Hymnal of the Second Temple." The last of the psalms were certainly written then—such as Psalm 137, which refers to the Babylonian captivity. Most importantly, however, it was during the second Temple period that the Psalter found its final form as a single book arranged in a very deliberate way.

How was it arranged? As we have it today, the Psalter falls into five segments or "books." Book I includes Psalms 1-41;

Book II, Psalms 42-72; Book III, Psalms 73-89; Book IV, Psalms 90-106; and Book V, Psalms 107-150. The ancient rabbis believed that the Psalter's division reflected the division of the Torah, the first five books of the Bible. Says the *Midrash Tehillim*, the oldest surviving commentary on the Psalms: "Moses gave Israel the five books [of the Law], and David gave Israel the five books of the Psalms." As the Law represented God's covenant with Moses, so the songs represented God's covenant with David.

Each "book" of the Psalter ends with a doxology, a brief verse or two blessing the Lord. Book I concludes with: "Blessed be the LORD, the God of Israel, from everlasting to everlasting! Amen and Amen" (Ps. 41:13). Each succeeding book closes with similar words (cf. Ps. 72:18-19; 89:52; 106:48). Psalm 150, which is six verses long, serves as a more expansive doxology to the fifth book and the entire Psalter; but, if that's not expansive enough, some commentators have seen the final five psalms, 146-50, as the book's concluding doxology.

The five-part division makes for a neat symmetry between the Psalter and the Torah; yet it does not tell us the "story" within the Psalter; nor does it tell us how the individual psalms found their way into one book or another. For the compiler (or compilers) did not arrange the psalms by author; David's compositions, for example, are spread throughout all five books. The psalms of the Sons of Korah appear in Books II and III, but are interspersed with those by other authors. Hebrew scholars point out that Books II and III are also marked by a tendency to address God by His generic name *Elohim* (God) rather than His personal name *Yahweh* (Lord). Still, this does not tell us why the psalms are divided as they are.

Nor can we say that the compiler separated the psalms according to liturgical purpose or literary form. Most of the psalms bear titles ("inscriptions") that include technical terms for their particular poetic forms: *miktam, shiggaion, maskil,* and others. (The meaning of the terms is unknown to us today.) Yet these forms, too, are dispersed through the Psalter, in no apparent order.

What, then, is the story within the Psalter? The question has occupied some of the best minds and souls in the history of biblical exegesis. Ancient and medieval Christians proposed an array of possible answers. Through much of the twentieth century, however, the question itself fell out of fashion, as scholars focused their attention on smaller and smaller portions of text. In psalm scholarship, literary form was the rage. Now the question has arisen again in academic circles, especially those influenced by "canonical criticism"—which emphasizes the study of texts within their traditional context. Let's look at some of the story lines discerned in the Psalter by careful readers of the Bible, ancient and modern.

The Several-Storied Psalter

In the sequence of psalms, some readers find a gradual movement from predicament to praise. After two brief introductory psalms, the early books of the Psalter tend to concentrate upon deliverance from dire circumstances. In contrast, most of the later psalms are songs of praise. Indeed, "songs of praise" is one literal way to translate the words "hallel psalms." From these last psalms we get the word *Halleluia*—which is Hebrew for "Praise the Lord!" The Hebrew title of the Psalter might provide further confirmations of this dramatic movement. Why call the book *Sefer Tehillim*, the "Book of Praises," if most of the praise is loaded at the end? It makes sense, say these readers, only if praise is the goal of the whole book—if praise is the fruit even of the psalmists' early difficulties.

Others see in the Psalter a first-person history of the rise and fall of the royal house of David and the ultimate enthronement of Yahweh as sole King of Israel. The Book of Psalms begins with confident songs of Davidic kingship, but then proceeds to lament the monarch's personal sin and the evil this sin has visited upon himself and his kingdom. Eventually, the ten northern tribes rebel and Israel divides into two kingdoms. Weakened, both kingdoms, Judah and Israel, are overrun by Gentile armies and the people carried off to exile. Yet, in the end, these seemingly tragic circumstances teach the people to rely on the Lord God as the only king who can triumph over all adversities. Thus, in this reading, the Psalter ends with praise of Yahweh's kingship over Israel and all the universe.

Still others see the Psalter as an allegory of the moral life. Saint Gregory of Nyssa (c. 335-95) discerned in the five books the growth of the soul through five stages of virtue, from initial conversion to final blessedness. The psalmist sets the agenda, said Gregory, with the first lines of the first psalm:

> Blessed is the man, who [1] walks not in the counsel of the wicked, [2] nor stands in the way of sinners, [3] nor sits in the seat of scoffers; but [4] his delight is in the law of the Lord, and [5] on his law he meditates day and night (Ps. 1:1-2).

Gregory traces the soul's progress, first as it turns away from sin, then as it detaches itself from passions and earthly attachments, and finally as it turns completely to God in contemplation. This final blessedness—beatitude—is a life begun on earth that will reach its perfection in heaven.

Christo-Clarity

Among Christian commentators, however, the overwhelming conviction is that the story of the Psalter is Christological: The Psalter, they say, is about Christ. Said Pope John Paul II in the first of his series of reflections on the Psalms (March 28, 2001):

The Fathers of the Church emphasized that the mystery of Christ is the key to understanding the Psalms. In the Psalms we contemplate the saving deeds of God in creation and history. They speak not only of the individual person of Christ but of the total Christ, composed of Christ the head and the members of His body.

This is the conviction of a majority of the Fathers of the Church, including Saint Justin Martyr, Saint Cyprian, Saint Hippolytus, Origen, Saint Athanasius, Eusebius, Saint Jerome, Saint Ambrose, Saint Augustine, Cassiodorus, and many others. Augustine went so far as to say that Psalm 22 alone "describes [the Passion of Christ] with all the evidence of a Gospel." Jerome held that certain psalms could be held as true of no one else but Jesus Christ. The Second Council of Constantinople in 553 denounced the prominent exegete Theodore of Mopsuestia precisely because he denied the messianic content of certain psalms.

This early Christological reading finds further confirmation in the texts of the most ancient liturgies. In the patristic era, Psalm 34—with the refrain, "O taste and see that the Lord is good!"—was almost universally employed as a Communion hymn. And the Christological reading was hardly a passing fad. Centuries after the age of the Fathers, Saint Thomas Aquinas deemed the Psalter to be "almost Gospel."

The Christological reading of the Psalter fell on hard times, however, in the nineteenth and twentieth centuries, when the historical-critical method was ascendant among academics. The *New Jerome Biblical Commentary*, for example, devoted thirty pages of small print to the Psalms without ever mentioning Tradition's overwhelmingly Christological interpretation.

Scholars have their reasons, of course, for rejecting the Tradition. Put simply, many think it wrong to read Christian theology back into pre-Christian Jewish texts. Some go so far as to say that a Christological interpretation does violence to the original authors' intentions. I disagree. And, though their arguments merit detailed and thoughtful response, I must leave that to other books. I have space here to raise just two objections—one theological and one historical—to those who reject (or ignore) the Christological reading of the Psalter.

Object Lessons

Sacred Tradition calls us to discover Christ in the Old Testament texts. Scripture demonstrates the Christological reading; Tradition confirms it; and the Church's Magisterium validates it for every age.

According to the Church Fathers, the truths of the Incarnation, the Redemption, and the Church were already present "in mystery" from the first moments of the Old Covenant. For the events of Jesus' life did not arise out of nothing. God had been preparing each of them from all eternity. To see Christ in the Old Testament, then, is to discern, with 20/20 hindsight, the workings of divine providence.

Jesus Himself read the Old Testament this way. He referred to Jonah (Mt. 12:39), Solomon (Mt. 12:42), the Temple (Jn. 2:19), and the brazen serpent (Jn. 3:14) as signs pointing to His own life, death, and Resurrection. Toward the end of Luke's Gospel, Jesus began with "Moses and all the prophets" and interpreted for His disciples what referred to Him "in *all* the scriptures" (Lk. 24:27). Saint Paul followed His Master in this reading of the Old Testament (cf. Rom. 5:14, Gal. 4:24), as did Saint Peter (cf. 1 Pet. 3:20-21).

This approach prevailed throughout the centuries, even in places like ancient Antioch, where biblical schools emphasized the literal-historical meaning of Old Testament texts. Origen, in third-century Alexandria, wrote extensively on the pervasive unity of the two Testaments. Saint Augustine—whose longest exegetical work is his *Expositions on the Psalms*—summed up this interpretive method in one sentence: The New Testament is concealed in the Old, and the Old is revealed in the New.

The historical reasons for preserving the Christological reading of the Psalter are as compelling as the theological reasons. For the Tradition is not merely a projection of Christian theology onto non-Christian texts. It is, rather, an organic development, an uninterrupted continuation, of the *Jewish* exegesis of Jesus' contemporaries.

The Jews of the first century (and the preceding five centuries) lived in intense anticipation of the arrival of God's Messiah, the Redeemer who would restore the Davidic kingship in Jerusalem over the reunited twelve tribes of Israel. Messiah (*Meshiach*) is Hebrew for "anointed"; its Greek equivalent is *Christos*—in English, *Christ*.

Consider the situation of Judaism during the time of the second Temple. Though a remnant of the tribes of Judah and Benjamin had returned to the land, ten tribes of Israel remained in dispersion among the Gentiles. Even the tribes that had been restored could hardly glory in their fortunes. The Temple itself was a mere shadow of what it once had been, and its Holy of Holies was empty, as the ark of the covenant had not been recovered since the Babylonian invasion. Moreover, through most of the second Temple period, the Jews were ruled by a succession of foreign powers: Persian, Greek, and Roman.

Who could rescue Israel from this seemingly impossible predicament? Only a man chosen, empowered, and protected by God. Even though David's line was apparently snuffed out at the time of the captivity (cf. 2 Kings 25:7), the Jews never ceased hoping for God's miraculous intervention in their history. For the Lord had promised David that a king in his line would one day rule all the nations, and he would reign forever.

> I will raise up your offspring after you, who shall come forth
> from your body, and I will establish his kingdom. . . . I will
> be his father, and he shall be my son (2 Sam. 7:12, 14).

In the centuries before Christ, there were many pretenders
to the title of Messiah, and most of them met a bad end, but
the people continued hoping. The messianic reading of the
Old Testament was commonplace with Jews living in the lands
of Israel as well as in the dispersion. This is evident in even a
cursory reading of the intertestamental literature: the *Book of
Enoch*, the *Testaments of the Twelve Patriarchs*, the *Sibylline
Oracles*, and especially the Dead Sea Scrolls.

Yet nothing evoked the longing of Israel so much as the
Psalter. The Psalms everywhere embodied the hope of God's
promises to David—the hope of a kingship that lasts forever,
of a universal kingdom, of the restoration of Israel's twelve
tribes, and of a holy city restored with a glorious Temple at its
heart. These promises, expressed repeatedly in the Psalms,
nourished the Jewish hope for the Messiah, who would be—
like Solomon—a royal son of David, as well as a priest forever
in the line of Melchizedek.

As liturgical hymns, the Psalms were profoundly effective in
sustaining Israel's culture—a culture of messianic expectation—
through a millennium, in spite of wars, exile, moral decay,
political upheaval, and foreign domination. The Psalms told
and retold the story of God's covenants with His people. They
renewed a climate of expectation, even as their liturgies
renewed the people's covenant with God.

This is the historical record. Israel's own reading of the
Psalter was messianic, and therefore Christological. Nor
can anyone claim that such findings are merely a Christian-
revisionist reading of history; they are central, for example,
to the work of non-Christian scholars such as Yale's Paula
Fredriksen, who is an Orthodox Jew.

If theology urges us toward a messianic reading of the Psalms, then history, for its part, shows that such a reading is hardly a Christian innovation.

Jesus' Hymn Self

Because they were songs, because they were poems, the Psalms served as the most useful means of transmitting culture. They were memorable, and so they were easily quotable. Philo of Alexandria, the great Jewish biblical scholar of the first century A.D., quotes the Psalter more than any other book in the Old Testament, except for the books of the Law. In the New Testament, references to the Psalms even surpass references to the Torah. All told, 103 out of 150 psalms appear in the pages of the New Testament, and many are quoted more than once.

Jesus' self-understanding draws deeply from the Psalms. The Letter to the Hebrews portrays Him as quoting the Psalms at the very moment of His Incarnation:

> [W]hen Christ came into the world, he said, "Sacrifices and offerings thou hast not desired, but a body hast thou prepared for me; in burnt offerings and sin offerings thou hast taken no pleasure." Then I said, "Lo, I have come to do thy will, O God" (Heb. 10:5-7; cf. Ps. 40:6-8).

In the last agony of His earthly life, Jesus quoted the Psalms twice from the Cross: "My God, my God, why hast thou forsaken me?" (Mt. 27:46; Ps. 22:1) and "Father, into thy hands I commit my spirit!" (Lk. 23:46; Ps. 31:5). In between that first moment and the last, Jesus invoked the Psalms at key events throughout His public ministry, including the Sermon on the Mount. At the climax of Jesus' confrontation with His opponents, He silenced them by His skillful use of Psalm 110 (cf. Mt. 22:43-46).

The Psalms remained important to the Christian generations immediately after the composition of the New Testament. For Jesus' followers believed that He was the Messiah, the Son of David. They believed that the Church was the promised kingdom of restored Israel with the Gentiles. They believed that a New Jerusalem was set on high in heaven—a holy city invulnerable to captivity, invasion, intrigue, or corruption. In the earliest papal document we have (outside the Scriptures), Pope St. Clement I, writing in the 90s, cited the Psalms almost fifty times in the course of a single letter. Many of the Fathers wrote commentaries on the Psalms; Origen and Saint Jerome may have written three apiece! Saint Gregory of Nyssa reported that, in the fourth century, the Psalms were sung everywhere and by everyone—"whether walking, at sea, or engaged in sedentary activities . . . [by] men and women, healthy and ill." Saint Jerome wrote that, in his day, farmers in the fields sang the Psalms while they were working.

I don't mean to romanticize the early Church. Despite all the familiarity with the Psalter, Saint John Chrysostom was still able to complain that "those singing it daily and uttering the words by mouth do not enquire about the force of the ideas underlying the words." That, indeed, was the reason Bishop Theodoret of Cyrus wrote his commentary on the Psalter: "so that they might sing its melodies and at the same time recognize the sense of the words they sing, thus reaping a double dividend."

What were the "underlying ideas" that made the Psalter as popular with the New Israel as it had been with the Old? For Christians, the Psalms were about Christ; He was the main character in the book. Spiritual writers would see Him present in the Psalms on several levels: The Psalms were the prayers of Christ; they were prayers to Christ; and they were prayers about Christ. But, if Christ was the character, what was the story? What was the big idea?

The story we've been trying to discern—the story within the Psalter—was the same for God's chosen people, the Jews, as it would be for His New Israel, the Church.

It is the story of the covenant.

The Real Story of the Psalter

"Covenant" is the idea that unites the two Testaments. A covenant, in ancient cultures, was a solemn agreement that created a family relation. Marriage was a covenant, as was the adoption of a child. When a family welcomed a new member, both parties would seal the covenant by swearing a sacred oath, sharing a common meal, and offering a sacrifice. The covenant brought with it certain blessings if the parties were faithful, and curses if they were not.

Nations used the legal form of a covenant when signing treaties. God used the form whenever He took a people as His own, as in His dealings with Adam, Noah, Abraham, Moses, and David. Consider the following passage from Yahweh's covenant with Moses and the Israelites:

> If you obey the commandments of the LORD your God which I command you this day, by loving the LORD your God, by walking in his ways, and by keeping his commandments . . . then you shall live and multiply, and the LORD your God will bless you in the land which you are entering to take possession of it. But if your heart turns away, and you will not hear, but are drawn away to worship other gods and serve them, I declare to you this day, that you shall perish; you shall not live long in the land. . . . I have set before you life and death, blessing and curse; therefore choose life, that you and your descendants may live (Deut. 30:16-19).

The terms of the relationship are clear; the consequences are clear. God's covenant with David would include similar terms.

In one sense, the Psalter tells the story of every covenant God has made with man. Its unique contribution is that it tells this story from the human perspective. We can read all the books of the Law and Prophets as God's terms for His covenant, but only the Psalms can we read as the human response.

In another sense, the Psalter tells the story of house of David in relation to the covenant. In still another sense, it tells the story of Christ, who came to establish a New Covenant in His blood (cf. Lk. 22:20). Yet the Psalter also tells the story of you and me, and of what happens if we are faithful to the New Covenant God has made with us, and what happens if we're not.

For the Psalter begins with a covenant blessing: "Blessed is the man . . ." and proceeds to enumerate the conditions of blessing. As the Book of Leviticus outlines the cultic and moral program for the Mosaic covenant, the Psalter outlines the cultic and moral program for the Davidic covenant, which included not only Israel but all the nations. "Clap your hands, all peoples! . . . For the LORD, the Most High, is . . . a great king over all the earth" (Ps. 47:1-2). The Psalter is a Davidic hymnal teaching all the nations how to address the God of Israel, how to know Him as a father, and how to discern His judgments in human life and human history. The covenant is the interpretive key.

Nor does the covenantal reading invalidate any of the other readings of the Psalter. Indeed, it unites them.

Yes, the Psalter moves from predicament to praise. Man finds himself in predicaments because of his infidelity, but such suffering has a remedial purpose. That taste of "death" calls to mind the terms of the covenant, which can be restored through repentance. (So praise the Lord!)

Yes, the Psalter tracks the growth of the soul in virtue. We may even define virtue as the habitual keeping of the terms of the covenant.

Yes, the Psalter is the story of the house of David—its rise and fall, and Yahweh's enthronement over Israel. But that story is unthinkable without the covenant. Only the covenant can account for the rise of David. Only the covenant can account for the fall precipitated by the sins of Solomon. Only the covenant can account for the kingdom's restoration in Jesus Christ, the Son of David.

The covenant also helps us to comprehend the Psalter's most difficult passages—those that wish evil upon the psalmists' enemies (e.g., Ps. 109:6-13). These "imprecatory psalms" are surely among the most controversial passages in Scripture and have proven to be a stumbling block to some would-be Christians. Consider the apparent vindictiveness of Psalm 69:

> Let their own table before them become a snare; . . . Let their eyes be darkened, so that they cannot see; and make their loins tremble continually. Pour out thy indignation upon them, and let thy burning anger overtake them. May their camp be a desolation, let no one dwell in their tents (vv. 22-25).

Here we must recall that, in the universal vision of the Davidic covenant, all the enemies of Israel—even the Babylonians—are all potential brothers. The only true enemies are the unconvertible powers of evil. Inasmuch as Babylonians oppose the will of God, they stand in the Psalms as symbols of the sin we must uproot from our lives and from the world. Inasmuch as the Babylonians act as puppets of the devil, Israel can wish for temporal afflictions that will lead to their earthly enemies' conversion.

Nor is this attitude incompatible (as some critics have claimed) with the Gospel of Jesus Christ. We find the same principle at work in Saint Paul's First Letter to the Corinthians. In the fifth chapter, Paul speaks of a man in

Corinth who is living a wicked life and urges the Church to cut all ties with the man. Paul, for his part, has "already pronounced judgment in the name of the Lord Jesus on the man" (vv. 3-4). Indeed he goes so far as to urge the Corinthians:

> When you are assembled, and my spirit is present, with the power of our Lord Jesus, you are to deliver this man to Satan for the destruction of the flesh, that his spirit may be saved in the day of the Lord Jesus (vv. 4-5).

Remember, the covenant always sets both blessings and curses before man, and lets man do the choosing. Yet we should not look upon the curses as mere punishments. God intends them to be remedial, restorative, and redemptive. The suffering of the curses serves as a means to humility and repentance, and an occasion to return to covenant faithfulness. And that's exactly how it worked for Paul and Corinth. The offender repented and was reconciled (cf. 2 Cor. 2:1-11).

This Is the Day

All the meanings of the Psalter come together if we discern the one uniting principle behind the Psalter, and indeed behind all Scripture: the covenant. It's not that we can't enjoy the Psalter in parts. It's not that we can't pray the Psalms one by one. It's not that individual psalms can't evoke our sympathy.

But how much richer our experience will be when we see the parts more clearly in relation to the whole. There's something profoundly theological about the Psalter's meaning, and there's something profoundly historical about its realization. Indeed, we read some lines of the Psalms and wonder how they could ever be understood by non-Christians: "Man ate of the bread of the angels" (Ps. 78:25). How could that refer to anything but the Holy Eucharist?

We live in exciting times for the study of the Psalms. Scholars are just beginning to turn from the minutiae of literary forms and hypothetical historical backgrounds to see the grandeur of the Psalter itself as a work of tremendous religious and theological importance. Scholars are also just beginning to return to the Christological reading of the Psalms.

What you're about to read in Michael Barber's book is not only good, but it's new—it's new to all of us. Moreover, it's important. Yet it will not always be easy reading. As you move through Barber's research, you'll need to keep your Bible close at hand. You'll need to read and reread the Psalms. You'll need to reread portions of this book as well. Above all, you'll need to pray about what you read. I urge you, though, to persevere. The most difficult material in this book is the material that will prove most profitable for your interior life.

Read on, then. Read carefully; and read again. Most importantly, while you read this book, pray the Psalms.

Scott Hahn, Ph.D.
Steubenville, Ohio

✠ CHAPTER 1 ✠

PSALM BACKGROUND
TO STUDYING THE PSALTER

"Truth," Bertrand de Margerie says, "is the Trinity."[1] This is because the Trinity explains *who* God is, not just *what* God does. Thus, all theology must flow from this ultimate truth and all of the mysteries of faith, understood in its light.

The *Catechism of the Catholic Church* makes the distinction, therefore, between *theologia* and *oikonomia*. The *theologia* explains *who* God is (i.e., the Trinity), while the *oikonomia* explains *what* God does in history (such as the covenants with the Patriarchs and Israel, the Exodus, etc.). Through His work in history, especially through the covenants, God reveals to us who He is.

This is not all that different from our own experience with other human beings. A man might reveal his feelings for a woman by leaving her a bouquet of roses. We have all heard the phrase "actions speak louder than words," so we know that through our actions we truly reveal ourselves to other people.

At the same time, we also understand another person's actions much better once we come to truly know that person. The woman who received the roses will understand more clearly the other actions of the man who gave them to her. Before he gave them to her, she might have noticed that he acted quirky around her, but now she realizes that he is

---

[1] Bertrand de Margerie, *The Christian Trinity in History* (Petersham, MA: St. Bede's Publications, 1982), xvii.

nervous because he cares for her. She now knows why he blushes, why he laughs so hard at all her jokes, and why he is always offering to do her favors. After he reveals himself to her, she can better understand the things that he does.

The same is true for God. Not only do we come to know who God is through His actions in salvation history, but we also come to better understand His work in history once we come to know Him. This is what the Catechism teaches:

> Through the *oikonomia* the *theologia* is revealed to us; but conversely, the *theologia* illuminates the whole *oikonomia*. God's works reveal who he is in himself; the mystery of his inmost being enlightens our understanding of all his works. So it is, analogously, among human persons. A person discloses himself in his actions, and the better we know a person, the better we understand his actions (Catechism, no. 236).

God makes Himself known to us through what He does, yet after He has revealed Himself to us, we can then understand more deeply His dealings with man.

As the *theologia* reveals that God is Father, the *oikonomia* illuminates God's fatherly plan. In fact, *oikonomia* comes from "*oikos*," meaning house, and "*nomos*," meaning law. We can see, then, that the *oikonomia* describes the way God administers His household, the way He Fathers His family. Because of this, any study of theology must start from two primary poles: the Trinity and the Word of God.

The Holiest Family

In the Trinity we see God as Three Persons, forever united in life-giving love. The Father begets the Son and shares with Him His life in love. He gives to the Son all His attributes, so that the Son, like the Father, is eternal, almighty, all-knowing, and all-loving.

The Son, then, is the image of the Father. Yet, in being the Son, the image of the Father, the Son must be like the Father in all things—including imitating the Father's act of life-giving love. The Son cannot truly be the image of the Father if the Father is pouring His life into the Son and the Son gives nothing in return! The Son, therefore, pours Himself out in life-giving love back to the Father. Moreover, since the Father and the Son pour out Their very life in love, this love itself is personified in another Person, the Holy Spirit. To truly be a son, then, means to pour one's own life out in life-giving love. As we shall see, this is what God asks of all those he calls to divine sonship, including Adam, Israel, and David.

In all of this, we must emphasize that each of the Three Persons is eternal. God's inner life is outside of time. We cannot speak of the Father coming *before* the Son or the Spirit coming *after* the Father and the Son. The Three are united from all eternity in their act of life-giving love. This Trinity of life-giving divine Persons is what is described by the *theologia.*

Taking God at His Word

The second major starting point of theology must be Scripture, which recounts God's actions in history, the *oikonomia.* Scripture is the Word of God in the very words of God (DV 11). Because of this, Scripture is without error and "should be the very soul of sacred theology" (*ibid.*).

We must note here that Scripture cannot be understood apart from the Church's living Tradition or her teaching office. Indeed, the canon of Scripture, the Bible's table of contents, was formed for the express purpose of defining what could be read in the Church's liturgy, which is identified with the Church's Tradition.[2] Likewise, the teaching office of

---

[2] Yves Congar, *Tradition and Traditions* (San Diego: Basilica Press, 1966), 354. See also Pope Pius XII, Encyclical Letter On the Sacred Liturgy *Mediator Dei* (1947), no. 48.

the Magisterium was established by Christ so that Christians would have an authoritative interpreter of Scripture (cf. Mt. 16:18-19; 1 Tim. 3:15). Without the authority of the Church, Christians would have no way of knowing with certainty whether or not the Church had "canonized" the right books as Scripture. Hence, Scripture itself teaches that it is not the "sole" authority (2 Thess. 2:15).

Nonetheless, due to its inspired charism, Scripture is "privileged" and has a certain primacy. Hence, the Pontifical Biblical Commission speaks of the "referential language of Scripture."[3] In addition, Cardinal Ratzinger explains that the "normative theologians are the authors of Scripture,"[4] because the Bible is "the model of all theology."[5] All doctrine and dogma, then, must be understood as the Church's clarification of the truth conveyed in Scripture. Thus Cardinal Ratzinger explains that dogma is "nothing other than the Church's infallible interpretation of Scripture."[6]

Therefore, the two poles for doing theology properly are clearly seen: who God is, the Trinity (the *theologia*) and what God does in history (the *oikonomia*), as recorded in Scripture, the privileged channel of revelation. With this foundation we are now ready to embark on our task.

Set for the Psalms

This book will attempt to provide a biblical theology of the Psalter following the principles explained above. It will show how the historical hope for the restoration of the Davidic

---

[3] Cited in Scott Hahn, "Prima Scriptura," *The Church and the Universal Catechism: Proceedings from the Fifteenth Convention of the Fellowship of Catholic Scholars*, Rev. Anthony Mastroeni, ed. (Steubenville, OH: Franciscan University Press, 1992), 91.

[4] Cardinal Joseph Ratzinger, *Principles of Catholic Theology: Building Stones for a Fundamental Theology* (San Francisco: Ignatius Press, 1987), 321.

[5] *Ibid.*

[6] Cardinal Joseph Ratzinger, "Crisis in Catechesis," *Canadian Catholic Review*, 7 (1983): 178.

kingdom, as represented in the Psalter, was fulfilled in the coming of Jesus. This kingdom was the means by which God would extend His covenant family bond to all men. In doing so God would restore man to the original calling that Adam received: divine sonship.

The book is divided into two parts. In Part I, we will first look at the Davidic covenant, seeing how it represents the climax of all of God's Old Testament promises. Then, we will examine Book of Psalms from a bird's-eye view, looking at the major themes represented in the Psalter. In the last section of Part I, we will take an in-depth look at the Psalter itself—a worm's eye view—looking at how the individual psalms and the subtle movement of the Psalter as a whole underscore the hope of the restoration of the Davidic kingdom.

Part II will show how Christ brings fulfillment to Israel's hopes. First, we will see how Christ restores the covenants that were partially fulfilled in the Davidic kingdom. Then, we will examine the kingdom as a central theme of Christ's earthly ministry. Finally, we will see how the Church constitutes the restoration of the kingdom through her sacramental life, especially the Eucharistic liturgy, and gathers all peoples and nations into God the Father's loving embrace.

✡ PART I ✡

A THEOLOGY OF
THE PSALTER

CHAPTER 2

THE DAVIDIC KINGDOM AS OLD TESTAMENT CLIMAX

An I for an I

Covenants make families. By means of a covenant, family ties can be extended. Through a covenant anyone may be adopted into a family as a son and a brother. Covenant scholar Paul Kalluveettil explains that "a covenant implies an adoption into the household, an extension of kinship, the making of a brother."[1]

While contracts simply involve the exchange of goods, covenants involve the exchange of persons.[2] In a covenant, one gives oneself to another:

> The idea, "I am yours, you are mine" underlines every covenant declaration. This implies a quasi-familial bond which makes sons and brothers. The act of accepting the other as one's own reflects the basic idea of covenant: an attempt to extend the bond of blood beyond the kinship

---

[1] Paul Kalluveettil, *Declaration and Covenant: A Comprehensive Review of Covenant Formulae from the Old Testament and the Ancient Near East* (Rome: Biblical Institute Press, 1982), 205. Scott Hahn, *Kinship by Covenant: A Biblical Theological Study of Covenant Types and Texts in the Old and New Testaments* (Ann Arbor, MI: UMI Dissertation Services, 1995), 656: "[T]he inner logic of the covenant is to be found in the solidarity and life-giving love of the family. . . ."

[2] Scott Hahn, *A Father Who Keeps His Promises: God's Covenant Love in Scripture* (Ann Arbor, MI: Charis Books, 1998), 26: "Another major difference between contracts and covenants may be discovered in their very distinctive forms of exchange. A contract is the exchange of property in the form of goods and services ('That is mine and this is yours'); whereas a covenant calls for the exchange of persons ('I am yours and you are mine'). . . ."

sphere, or, in other words, to make a partner one's own flesh and blood . . . covenant is relational.[3]

From this it is clear that a covenant implies an "interpersonal communion," or gift of self.

God's covenant with David plays an important role in salvation history. It represents the fullest realization of His plan to restore covenantal/familial bonds with all of mankind. To better understand the Davidic covenant, let us briefly look at the three main covenants preceding it—the Adamic, the Abrahamic, and the Israelitic.

In the Beginning

In the seven-day creation narrative, we already find covenant imagery. The Hebrew word for swearing an oath is *sheba*, which literally means "to seven-oneself." Hence, the world is created in covenant relationship with God: It is made in seven days. The sign of this covenant is the Sabbath (cf. Ex. 20:10-11).[4]

From the outset, God creates man in covenant relationship. By virtue of this covenant, Adam is the recipient of divine sonship (cf. Lk. 3:38). This can be seen from the description of Adam as created in the "image" and "likeness" of God (Gen. 1:26). Later on we read that Seth is begotten in the "image" and "likeness" of Adam (Gen. 5:3).[5] From this we can see that the phrase "image and likeness" implies sonship.[6]

---

[3] Kalluveettil, *Declaration and Covenant*, 212.

[4] Pope John Paul II, Apostolic Letter On Keeping the Lord's Day Holy *Dies Domini*, no. 8 (Boston: Pauline Books and Media, 1998), 18: "According to the priestly writer of the first biblical creation story, then was born the 'Sabbath,' so characteristic of the first Covenant, and which in some ways foretells the sacred day of the new and final Covenant."

[5] What is interesting here is that in the Septuagint the word for Seth's likeness is different from the one used for Adam in Genesis 2. Adam is made after God's "likeness" (ὁμοίωσις), but Seth is begotten after Adam's "form" (ἰδέα). This may be related to Catechism, no. 705, which tells us that man disfigured the image of God within him, but lost the likeness.

[6] Leander Keck *et al.*, eds., *The New Interpreter's Bible*, vol. 1 (Nashville, TN:

Closely linked to Adam's sonship is his role as priest. This sacred service is implied when God tells Adam that he is to "keep" the garden (Gen. 2:15). The word for "keep" or "guard" in Hebrew, *shamar*, implies priestly duties.[7] Likewise, the word for "tilling" the garden in Genesis 2:15 (*'abad*) also implies worship.

Furthermore, the world may be understood as one huge temple.[8] Genesis presents God's creation of the world in terms of temple building. This interpretation is underscored by many historical-critical scholars who, upon seeing this emphasis, ascribe to it the "priestly" tradition. Thus, the construction of the tent of God's dwelling and, later, the Temple itself are patterned after the creation account. Cardinal Ratzinger explains: "Seven times it says, 'Moses did as the Lord had commanded him,' words that suggest the seven-day work on the tabernacle replicates the seven-day work on creation."[9] Likewise, the construction of the Temple took seven years and was dedicated after a seven-day feast (Tabernacles), in the seventh month, with a seven-part prayer.[10]

If the world is the Temple, the garden is the sanctuary. The intertestamental Book of Jubilees explains: "[Noah] knew that the garden of Eden was the Holy of Holies and the dwelling

---

Abingdon Press, 1994), 380: "The relationship between son and father embodies the notion of image."

[7] Meredith Kline, *Kingdom Prologue* (South Hamilton, MA: M.G. Kline, 1993), 54: "Elsewhere in the Bible, especially in passages dealing with the functions of the priests and Levites in Israel, the verb *shamar* occurs frequently in the sense of guarding the holiness of God's sanctuary against profanation by unauthorized 'strangers' (cf., e.g., Num. 1:53; 3:8, 10, 32; 8:26; 18:3ff.; 31:30, 47; 1 Sam. 7:1; 2 Kings 12:9; 1 Chron. 23:32; 2 Chron. 34:9; Ezek. 44:15f., 48:11)."

[8] Meredith Kline, *Images of the Spirit* (Eugene, OR: Wipf and Stock Publishers, 1998), 39.

[9] Cardinal Joseph Ratzinger, *The Spirit of the Liturgy* (San Francisco: Ignatius Press, 2000), 26-27.

[10] Jon D. Levenson, *Sinai and Zion: An Entry into the Jewish Bible* (Minneapolis: Winston Press, 1985), 143-44.

of the Lord."[11] Like the Holy of Holies, the garden was oriented toward the east.[12] Moreover, a cherub was the guardian of the garden, just as the ark of the covenant in the Holy of Holies was overshadowed by the two cherubim. Yet another link between the garden and the Temple is the fact that both of them contained gold and onyx.[13]

Adam's role as priest should be understood in relation to his divine sonship. Before the golden calf incident, first-born sons functioned as priests in Israel. Rabbi Brichto concludes: "There is ample evidence that the role of priest in the Israelite family had at one time been fulfilled by the first born."[14] Thus, in Numbers 3 a census is taken of the first-born and then of the Levites, showing this replacement: "And the LORD said to Moses, 'Take the Levites instead of all the first-born among the people of Israel . . ." (Num. 3:44-45). Milgrom explains, "The replacement of the first-born by the Levites implies that the former originally held sacred status."[15] This idea is also found in rabbinic tradition.

In fact, even after the golden calf incident, the priesthood of first-born sons was still widespread. Judges 17:5 tells us how Micah installed his own son to be a priest in the absence of a Levite. There is, therefore, a relationship between sonship and priesthood.

---

[11] Jubilees 8:19. See James Charlesworth, ed., *The Old Testament Pseudepigrapha*, vol. 2 (New York: Doubleday, 1998), 73.

[12] See Warren Austin Gage, *The Gospel of Genesis* (Winona Lake, IN: Carpenter Books, 1984), 57.

[13] Hahn, *A Father Who Keeps His Promises*, 55. The Holy of Holies was also decorated with palm trees and flowers which also demonstrated its link with the garden. See Gage, *The Gospel of Genesis*, 57.

[14] Cited in Hahn, *Kinship by Covenant*, 216.

[15] Jacob Milgrom, *The JPS Torah Commentary: Numbers* (Philadelphia: Jewish Publication Society, 1990), 17. Milgrom goes on to say: "Thus the Bible may be preserving a memory of the first-born bearing sacred status; his replacement by the Levites may reflect the establishment of a professional, inherited priestly class" (18).

However, just as Adam is presented in priestly terms, he is also presented as a king. One scholar, Meredith Kline, finds several terms which indicate Adam's kingship, including his dominion, his call to subjugate the earth, and his naming of creatures.[16] Psalm 8 exemplifies the kingship of Adam, saying that God has "crowned him with glory and honor" and "given him dominion," putting "all things under his feet" (Ps. 8:6).

Adam, therefore, was a priest-king. Yet, his kingship needed to be subordinated to his priestly calling. Adam was to sanctify all creation and bring it into the seventh-day rest as an offering to God. Peter Leithart explains: "[Adam and Eve] were to go about their royal tasks for six days, only to return at the end of the week to offer themselves and their works to the Lord."[17]

Leithart explains Adam's sacrifice as consisting of his offering of self. In fact, by refusing to make this self-offering, Adam failed the covenant. Let us examine this more carefully.

Garden-Variety Snake?

Earlier we saw that Adam was told to guard (*shamar*) the garden. In other words, he was given the priestly duty of guarding the sanctuary of Eden from an invader, i.e., Satan.[18] Furthermore, Adam was supposed to defend his wife. Genesis teaches us that Adam and Eve were created in covenant with one another. The deep sleep that God put Adam into indicates

---

[16] See Kline, *Kingdom Prologue*, 25: "Man is located in [Genesis 1-3] as king over all the created order of the six days."

[17] Peter J. Leithart, *The Kingdom and the Power* (Phillipsburg, NJ: Presbyterian & Reformed Publishing, 1993), 28.

[18] *Ibid.*: "The conclusion appears warranted, therefore, that Genesis 2:15 contains an explicit reference to the entrusting of man in his priestly office with the task of defending the Edenic sanctuary against the intrusion of . . . the Satanic serpent." Hahn, *A Father Who Keeps His Promises*, 59: Adam's call to *shamar* "seemed to imply not only a need for the sanctity of the garden to be guarded but the existence of a potential intruder to desecrate it."

the passing of one night. This means that Adam awoke to find Eve on the seventh day. "So Adam's first full day may have been both a day of sabbath rest and betrothal, for Eve and himself, as marriage covenant partners."[19]

However, Adam failed to fulfill his covenant duties. When the serpent entered the garden, Adam stepped aside and did not guard the garden sanctuary or his wife from the evil it represented. To better appreciate Adam's silence, it is important to note that the Hebrew word for serpent, *nahash*, has deadly connotations. The same word is used in Numbers 21:6 to identify the fiery serpents that attacked Israel in the desert. *Nahash* is also used in Isaiah 27:1 to refer to Leviathan. Still also in Job 26:13 it is used to describe the sea monsters. And finally, in Revelation, the serpent of Genesis is depicted as a dragon:

> And another portent appeared in heaven; behold, a great red dragon, with seven heads and ten horns, and seven diadems upon his heads. His tail swept down a third of the stars of heaven, and cast them to the earth. And the dragon stood before the woman who was about to bear a child, that he might devour her child when she brought it forth; . . . And the great dragon was thrown down, that ancient serpent, who is called the Devil and Satan, the deceiver of the whole world—he was thrown down to the earth, and his angels were thrown down with him (Rev. 12:3-4, 9).

In this light, the "serpent" Adam faced should not be understood simply as a little snake, but rather as a powerful, supernatural creature capable of inflicting death.[20]

---

[19] Hahn, *A Father Who Keeps His Promises*, 63.
[20] In light of God's warning to Adam that should he eat of the tree of knowledge he would die, Adam must have known he was capable of dying, "since it would be senseless to threaten a man with a meaningless penalty. So while it isn't clear *how* Adam knew, it's reasonably certain *that* he did, at least in some way." *Ibid.*, 60 (original emphasis).

This seems to indicate that Adam was to enter into mortal combat with a creature more powerful than himself. Adam's failure to engage this demonic serpent in battle was the result of his unwillingness to lay down his life in defense of the garden sanctuary and his bride.[21] Thus, Adam failed to offer his life as a priestly sacrifice to God. Pride and fear of suffering, therefore, lay at the heart of the original sin. This is confirmed by Hebrews 2:14-15, which explains that Adam sinned because of his "fear of death."[22]

The ordeal of Adam, then, consisted in a choice between natural life or the life of grace. Adam was presented with the prospect of the greatest natural evil—the loss of earthly life. However, by clinging to the natural instinct of self-preservation and abandoning his divine calling, Adam lost something even greater than his earthly life—the life of grace in his soul. As Jesus said, "He who loves his life loses it, and he who hates his life in this world will keep it for eternal life" (Jn. 12:25). Had Adam sought to order his will to God's, he would have been given wisdom which would have helped him understand that the loss of natural life would be a lesser evil than the loss of the life of grace.

Hence, Proverbs calls wisdom the "tree of life" (Prov. 3:18), because the tree of life shows us that earthly life is not the ultimate prize. This also explains why a tree of life would be

---

[21] The idea that Adam was to defend Eve in mortal combat against the serpent is evident in the pseudepigrapha (anonymous Jewish religious writings of the period 200 B.C. to 200 A.D.). After God banished Adam and Eve from the garden, the book called the "First Book of Eden" (or "The Conflict of Adam and Eve with Satan") records several battles between Adam and the serpent in which the serpent tried to kill the first man and his wife. One such example is found in chapter 18: "When the accursed serpent saw Adam and Eve it swelled its head, stood on its tail, and with eyes blood-red, did as if it would kill them. It made straight for Eve, and ran after her. . . ." See Frank Crane, ed., *The Bible and the Forgotten Books of Eden* (Newfoundland: World Bible Publishers, 1927), 14.

[22] This is the passage used by the Council of Trent to describe the fall. See Council of Trent, Session V, Decree Concerning Original Sin, art. 1.

needed in the garden. If Adam's natural life would not be threatened, why would God place a tree of life in the garden? Obviously, the tree itself signals the mortal danger of Adam's trial.

In summary, God willed to give His grace to humanity through Adam, and this gift was contingent upon Adam's willingness to prefer the good of grace to the natural goods of this life. Adam was a priest-king whose sacrifice consisted in freely offering not only that which he had dominion over, but also himself. In doing so, Adam would have realized his status as God's son—offering his life in return for the divine life of grace.

Binding Promises

Now let us consider the Abrahamic covenant. God's covenant with Abraham partially reversed the curses of the Adamic covenant.[23] Whereas Adam failed by disobedience, Abraham acted faithfully.

In Genesis 12, God called Abram and gave him a threefold promise of (1) land, (2) a great name, and (3) offspring. These promises were then solemnified by covenant oaths in chapters 15, 17, and 22. These covenants prefigure the deliverance of Israel from Egypt and their inheritance of the Promised Land, the Davidic dynasty, and the New Covenant blessing extending to all the nations.[24]

There is a certain narrowing of the covenant promise from Genesis 12 onwards. God promises Abram an heir in Genesis 15:4 and that his descendants will receive the land from the river of Egypt to the river Euphrates (cf. Gen. 15:18). However, this greatly exceeds the borders of the "Promised Land" entered by Israel under Joshua. This land includes Arabia.

---

[23] Hahn, *Kinship by Covenant*, 540.
[24] *Ibid.*, 186-87.

In Genesis 16, Abram has relations with his concubine, Hagar, who conceives Ishmael. God then promises to greatly multiply Hagar's descendants through her son (cf. Gen. 16:10). However, in chapter 17, God changes Abram's name to Abraham, and informs him that Ishmael will not be his heir, but that his wife's son, Isaac, shall be the one through whom His covenant promise will be fulfilled. Hence, we have two lines of descent—one through Isaac, the Israelites, and one through Ishmael, the father of the Arabs.[25] This explains why Israel does not receive all of the land promised in Genesis 15:18.

It also explains why in Genesis 17, God's promise of the land to Abraham's appointed heir, Isaac, is limited to the land of Canaan. Interestingly, we further discover that the land of Canaan is also the land of the Edomites, Ammonites, and the Moabites—relatives of Abram.[26] Later, we will see how this is important to understanding the kingdom of David, as David does not seek to remove those peoples from the land that God has promised them.

We also see a movement from nationhood to kingdom in Genesis 17. In chapter 15, God promises to deliver Abraham's descendants, including Israel, from bondage.[27] Yet, God's

---

[25] Jubilees 20:12: "And Ishmael and his sons . . . dwelt from Paran to the entrance to Babylon in all of the land which faces east opposite the desert . . . and they are called Arabs or Ishmaelites." Charlesworth, *The Old Testament Pseudepigrapha*, vol. 2, 94. See also Karl-Josef Kuschel, *Abraham: Sign of Hope for Jews, Christians and Muslims* (New York: Continuum, 1995), 136: "Granted, the Bible does not know the term 'Arabs,' but we must assume that the area of settlement indicated here is the north-western desert of Arabia. Moreover, the historical reliability of the biblical accounts is reinforced by other sources, since the tribes of Ishmael mentioned in Genesis regularly appear as Arab tribes in Assyrian inscriptions from different times. . . . So it is not surprising that later Jewish tradition made Ishamel directly the father of the Arabs."

[26] Ammon and Moab are born through paternal incest to Lot (cf. Gen. 19:30-38), the nephew of Abram (Gen. 11:28), while Edomites are the descendants of Esau, Isaac's brother. Deuteronomy 2:1-37 describes these peoples in fraternal terms.

[27] It is important to note that Israel—that is, the descendants of Jacob—are not the only ones delivered from bondage in Egypt. The Hebrews—all the descendants of Eber (cf. Gen. 11:10-30)—are delivered. See Exodus 9:1.

promise in Genesis 17:6, "kings shall come forth from you," is fulfilled in the Davidic kingdom.[28]

Finally, in Genesis 22, we read the climactic covenant promise made to Abraham—that all nations will be blessed through him. However, this promise is only sworn after a kind of covenant ordeal, whereby, like Adam's trial, the offering of self is the prerequisite. In what ancient commentators have called the story of the "Aqedah"—referring to the "binding" of Isaac—God commands Abraham to sacrifice his only son on Mount Moriah as a holocaust. Though an angel is sent to stop Abraham from killing his son, Abraham's willingness to sacrifice his beloved son proves his fidelity.

On one level, this sacrifice constitutes a self-offering on the part of Abraham. Even though Isaac is the one to be offered, this is clearly a sacrifice of self for Abraham, who would have gladly offered himself in Isaac's place. Yet, on another level, the story of the Aqedah is a story of Isaac's willingness to offer himself as a sacrifice to God. Isaac's ability to carry the wood of the sacrifice up the mountain seems to imply a grown youth, capable of stopping an aged, decrepit Abraham from tying him down and killing him. In fact, the ancient Jewish historian Josephus says Isaac was twenty-five.[29] To many ancient commentators, the consent of Isaac is primary to the meaning of the story. Therefore, Abraham partially reverses Adam's failure to be a life-giving lover. God's oath to bless all nations, extending His covenant relationship to them, is given because of this willingness to self-sacrifice.[30]

---

[28] It is important to note that the promise of Genesis 17 is phrased in future terminology. See Hahn, *Kinship by Covenant*, 188.

[29] Antiquities Book I, section 13, no. 2. *The Works of Josephus: New Updated Edition*, William Whiston, trans. (Peabody, MA: Hendrickson Publishers, 1987), 43.

[30] For a fuller treatment of the willingness of Isaac in the story of the Aqedah, see James L. Kugel, *The Bible As It Was* (Cambridge, MA: Belknap Press, 1997), 174-75.

One Nation Under God

The last of the three major covenants we shall examine is God's covenant with Israel. However, as with Abraham, it is important to distinguish the different covenants within this relationship. Israel was a nation consisting of twelve tribes descended from Abraham's grandson, Jacob. Once Israel was delivered from Egypt, the twelve tribes entered into a covenant with God. God declared that Israel was His "first-born son" among the nations (Ex. 4:22-23) and wanted to make them a "kingdom of priests" (Ex. 19:6), through whom all nations would be blessed by God.[31] God would thereby fulfill His promise to Abraham. This covenant was established as Moses took the blood of bulls and sprinkled it on the people, who swore: "All that the LORD has spoken we will do" (Ex. 24:7).

Only a few days later, Israel broke the covenant by erecting a golden calf. Though Israel deserved death for breaking the covenant, God could not kill Israel without violating His unconditional oath to bless the nations through Abraham's seed.[32] Instead, Israel was put on probation under the Levites, who were employed as temporary priests in the place of the first-born sons and who were meant to rehabilitate Israel through the teaching of the Holiness Code.[33]

When the next generation sinned again at Baal-Peor, it was clear that Israel was far from cured. God then gave Israel the law of Deuteronomy, a lesser covenant given because of Israel's

---

[31] Chris Wright, *Knowing Jesus Through the Old Testament* (London: Marshall Pickering, 1999), 86: "God assigns his people as a whole community the role of priesthood for the nations. As their priests stood in relation to God and the rest of Israel, so they as a whole community were to stand in relation to God and the rest of the nations."

[32] See Hahn, *Kinship by Covenant*, 233-34.

[33] The role of the Levites is described in the *Testaments of the Twelve Patriarchs*. Levi tells his sons that the Lord has told him: "The light of knowledge you shall kindle in Jacob, and you shall be as the sun for all the posterity of Israel." Testament of Levi 4:3. See Charlesworth, *The Old Testament Pseudepigrapha*, vol. 1, 789.

hardness of heart.[34] This law was meant to show Israel its weakness so that it would acknowledge its inability to achieve holiness on its own, but rather needed God's help.[35] Whereas before Israel was called to go out to the nations to bring God's blessing to them, fulfilling God's promise to Abraham, Israel was now quarantined from them.

There is another element we must consider. Just as Adam failed to fulfill the covenant because of his fear of death, something similar happened to Israel. God had promised Israel that He would give them the land of Canaan. So Moses sent twelve spies into the land to develop a strategy for taking it back. Yet, when they returned from their mission, the spies scared Israel out of going up against those who dwelt in the land, telling the people that the inhabitants were "giants" who made them feel as small as "grasshoppers" (Num. 13:31-33).

So then, instead of heeding the Lord's call and engaging in mortal combat with those who had come into the land unlawfully,[36] Israel rejected the Lord, fearing the loss of life more than displeasing God. Because of their wickedness, the

---

[34] Ezekiel 20 describes this in great detail. First, in vv. 10-12, God recalls how He led Israel out of Egypt and made a covenant with them. Next, God describes how they rebelled against Him in the golden calf incident. Third, God explains how He did not destroy them because of the oath He swore to Abraham (v. 14). Then God remembers the failed attempt at restoring the covenant with the second generation (vv. 18-21). Finally, God tells how He gave this generation a law that "was not good"—i.e., Deuteronomy (v. 25). Jesus Himself, when explaining why Deuteronomy allowed for divorce, acknowledges the inferiority of the law, saying: "For your hardness of heart Moses allowed you to divorce your wives, but from the beginning it was not so" (Mt. 19:8).

[35] Saint Thomas Aquinas, *Summa Theologiae*, Ia IIae, q. 98, art. 2: "God sometimes permits certain ones to fall into sin, that they may be thereby be humbled. So also did He wish to give such a law as men by their own forces could not fulfill, so that, while presuming on their own powers, they might find themselves to be sinners, and being humbled might have recourse to the help of grace."

[36] Here we see another parallel with Adam. Just as the serpent did not rightfully belong in the garden, since Adam was to guard it from him, the Promised Land was inhabited by poachers, who were dwelling in the land already sworn to the descendants of Abraham.

people were banished to the desert until the first generation died out, much like Adam and Eve were banished from Eden after their sin. Here again we see a kind of trial by ordeal upon which God's blessing is contingent.

One Israelite of note is Phinehas. In Numbers 25, the second generation rebels as the first did with the golden calf. However, Phinehas stands out as a man willing to defend the sanctuary of God against those who would unlawfully enter it. Because of his faithfulness, God awards him the covenant of the perpetual priesthood. As a result, the high priest would be chosen from his descendants (cf. Num. 25:1-13). Just as the Levites replaced the first-born, so too, the descendants of Phinehas, the righteous priest, replaced the Levites.[37]

We have traced the development of God's covenant with mankind. First, we saw God's covenant extended to Adam, granting him divine sonship and making him a priest-king. However, Adam failed to keep the covenant because of his fear of suffering and death, thus triggering its curses.

We have also seen how God's desire to bring mankind back into His covenant family was advanced through the Abrahamic covenant. Cardinal Schönborn explains: "In the call of Abraham we see God's great plan at work: to gather together all mankind to be his family."[38] God promised Abraham that he would be the father of a great nation and that kings would come from him. Further, because of Abraham's willingness to offer his son Isaac, God promised to bless all mankind through his seed.

Israel, then, represents the covenant people through whom God will bless all nations. They entered into a covenant rela-

---

[37] Phinehas was a Levite. However, now the high priesthood is not given to all the sons of Aaron, but only the sons of Phinehas, Aaron's grandson. There is a narrowing of the priesthood here. See Hahn, *Kinship by Covenant*, 264-304.

[38] Cardinal Christoph Schönborn, *Loving The Church: Spiritual Exercises Preached in the Presence of Pope John Paul II* (San Francisco: Ignatius Press, 1998), 90.

tionship with God, making them a kingdom of priests who were to go to the nations and bring them back to God. However, Israel failed this covenant. God therefore gave them a "lower" law, which was meant to rehabilitate them. Notice the golden thread that runs throughout these covenants. Man must learn to become a life-giving lover—willing to suffer for God. Having surveyed these covenants, we can now better understand the significance of the Davidic covenant.

An Everlasting Kingdom

In 2 Samuel 7, we read about the establishment of the Davidic covenant. In this chapter there is a series of puns on the Hebrew word for "house": God promises David a dynasty (a "throne" or "royal house," v. 13) through an heir (a son— "house" here means family, v. 11) who will build a temple for Yahweh (the Lord's "house," v. 13).[39] Further, God swears to David's offspring the gift of divine sonship—"I will be his father, and he shall be my son" (v. 14). Finally, God promises that the Davidic throne will last forever (vv. 13-16).

Though 2 Samuel 7 makes no reference to a covenant *per se*, the fact that God's promise to David was ensured by a covenantal oath is clear from other passages in Scripture. In looking for references to the Davidic covenant, it is important to note that terms such as "swearing," "oath," and "decree" are covenant vocabulary. With this in mind we will examine Psalms 89, 110, and 132.

Psalm 89 is clearly based on the divine promise found in 2 Samuel 7.[40] It was composed after the fall of the Davidic

---

[39] See P.D. Miller, "Psalm 127—The House That Yahweh Builds," *Journal for the Study of the Old Testament*, 22 (1982), 119-32.

[40] The psalm alludes to Nathan's oracle to David, recorded in 2 Samuel 7 (as well as its parallel passage in 1 Chronicles 17). See Robert Cole, *The Shape and Message of Book III* (Psalms 73-89) (Sheffield, England: Sheffield Academic Press, 2000), 218: "Psalm 89 is a discussion not only of the Davidic covenant as expressed in Psalm 72 but also of its original form in 2 Samuel 7."

dynasty and cries out to God for its restoration.[41] The psalmist's lament is made on the basis of God's covenant oath to David.

The promises of the Davidic covenant are outlined more fully in this psalm than in 2 Samuel 7. Whereas 2 Samuel 7:14 provided that the Davidic king would be God's son, Psalm 89:27 calls him God's "first-born" son. While 2 Samuel 7:9 stated that the Davidic king would have a "great name, like the name of the great ones of the earth," Psalm 89:27 states that God will make him "the highest of the kings of the earth." Finally, Psalm 89 elaborates on the promise of an eternal throne, lengthening the promise to almost five verses, climaxing in verse 37: "Like the moon it shall be established for ever; it shall stand firm while the skies endure."[42]

Psalm 110 also highlights the importance of the God's oath to David. Alden shows a chiastic structure within the psalm:

A. v. 1 The Lord installs the king
   B. v. 2 He is sent out to conquer
      C. v. 3 The day of power
         D. v. 4 *The Lord swears a solemn oath*
      C.¹ v. 5 The day of wrath
   B.¹ v. 6 He goes out to conquer
A.¹ v. 7 The Lord installs the king[43]

Hence, the center of the psalm is the oath sworn to David.

It is also important to note the psalm's reference to the priestly role of the Davidic king: "You are priest for ever after

---

[41] Gerald Henry Wilson, *The Editing of the Hebrew Psalter* (Chico, CA: Scholars Press, 1985), 214: "Regardless of the guilt of the Davidic kings which brought on the punishment of the exile, surely YHWH must honor his covenant and re-establish the Davidic kingdom . . . And yet YHWH delays. It is this problem of the failure of YHWH to honor the Davidic Covenant that Psalm 89 depicts in its plea."

[42] See Craig Broyles, *New International Biblical Commentary: Psalms* (Peabody, MA: Hendrickson Publishers, 1999), 379.

[43] R.L. Alden, "Chiastic Psalms (III): A Study in the Mechanics of Semitic Poetry in Psalms 101-150," *Journal of Evangelical Theological Studies*, 21 (1978), 199-210.

the order of Melchizedek" (Ps. 110:4). While David's priestly status is not discussed in 2 Samuel 7, it is clearly demonstrated in 2 Samuel 6. There David offers sacrifice (v. 13), wears an ephod (the garment of a priest, v. 14), pitches the sacred tent and sacrifices in it (v. 17), blesses the people (v. 18), and distributes bread to the people (v. 19). In this last activity, David is like Melchizedek, who was also a bread-bringing priest-king in Jerusalem (cf. Ps. 110:4).[44] We will discuss this in more detail in Chapter 3.

The link between the bringing up of the ark to Jerusalem and the establishment of the Davidic dynasty in 2 Samuel 6-7 is made in Psalm 132. According to many scholars, Psalm 132 should be read against the backdrop of David's procession with the ark.[45] The psalm is divided into two parts: verses 1-10 and 10-18. Its internal structure is revealing:

A. v. 1-2 the sworn oath—of David's
   B. v. 3-8 God's habitation for rest and dwelling on Zion
      C. v. 9 priests clothed as the saints shout
         D. v. 10 David declared to be the Lord's anointed
A.¹ v. 11 the sworn oath—of Yahweh's
   B.¹ v. 12-15 God's habitation for rest and dwelling on Zion
      C.¹ v. 16 priests clothed as the saints shout
         D.¹ v. 17-18 David declared to be the Lord's anointed[46]

Thus, the psalm is marked by two oaths, David's and God's. The first part of the psalm recounts David's oath to bring up the ark to Jerusalem; the second deals with God's oath to David. Hence, the psalm teaches us that David's act of

---

[44] See Hahn, *Kinship by Covenant*, 312-19.
[45] Broyles, *New International Biblical Commentary*, 471; Mays, *Psalms*, 409; Hans-Joachim Kraus, *Theology of the Psalms* (Minneapolis: Augsburg Publishing House, 1986), 108.
[46] See Hahn, *Kinship by Covenant*, 330.

bringing up the ark, recorded in 2 Samuel 6, brought about God's covenant oath, narrated in 2 Samuel 7.[47]

The Davidic Covenant "in Deutero"

The Davidic covenant fulfills the conditions of the Deuteronomic covenant. First, we can see that Deuteronomy made provisions for a king.

> When you come to the land which the LORD your God gives you, and you possess it and dwell in it, and then say, "I will set a king over me, like all the nations that are round about me"; you may indeed set as king over you him whom the LORD your God will choose (Deut. 17:14-15).

David fulfills this provision. Hence, we see that David's kingship does not contradict God's.[48]

Second, in Deuteronomy Moses tells Israel that once they have attained "rest" from all their surrounding enemies, God will choose a place for His Name to dwell and, in that place, Israel will offer its sacrifices (Deut. 12:10-11). In 2 Samuel 7:1, David finally achieves this "rest" and therefore partially fulfills the requirements of the Deuteronomic covenant. Once David gains rest from his enemies, he desires to build the Temple.

Third, David fulfills in himself the original Sinai calling of Israel, receiving divine sonship and becoming a priest-king. This was originally the corporate calling of the Israelites, who were to be God's first-born sons and a kingdom of priests

---

[47] *Ibid.*, 338.

[48] Meredith Kline, *Treaty of the Great King* (Grand Rapids, MI: Eerdmans, 1963), 97: "Though the establishment of a monarchy is presented not as mandatory but as permissible, that is sufficient to show that a monarchy as such need not be antithetical to the principle of theocratic government." Later, this will be important in challenging the thesis that after Psalm 89 the Davidic throne is replaced by faith in God's kingship.

(Ex. 4:22-23; 19:6). Hence, "[t]he king's divine sonship may be seen as the perfection of the nation's."[49] Thus God's desire to extend divine sonship to mankind is fulfilled in David in a way not seen since Adam, because David is the first individual to receive this promise since the fall.

Fourth, the Davidic kingdom represents the extension of God's covenant, not only to Israel, but also to the nations. The Davidic kingdom fulfills the Abrahamic covenant as it allows a place for the Edomites, Ammonites, and Moabites, who were all promised the land through Abraham, as we saw before. Moreover, the Davidic kingdom includes a place for *all* the nations. Psalm 72 tells us that the Davidic king's reign extends to "the ends of the earth" so that "all nations serve him" (Ps. 72:8, 11). Through King David God partially fulfills His promise to bless all the nations. Echoing God's promise to Abraham, the psalmist tells us in reference to the king: "May men bless themselves by him, all nations call him blessed!" (Ps. 72:17). We will look at the international character of the Davidic covenant in more depth in the next chapter.

Fifth, the Davidic covenant represents a fulfillment inasmuch as the sons of Phinehas are finally elevated to the position of high priest through the Zadokites. As we saw earlier, the high priesthood was sworn to Phinehas' descendants in Numbers 25. However, not until King Solomon, the son of David, finally deposes Abiathar

	Aaron	
Eleazar		Ithamar
Phinehas[1]		?
Abishua		
Bukki		
Uzzi		
Zechariah		Eli
Meraioth		Phinehas[2]
Amariah		Ahitub[2]
Ahitub[1]		Ahimelech
Zadok		Abiathar

[49] Hahn, *Kinship by Covenant*, 359.

and installs Zadok as sole high priest is the covenant with Phinehas fulfilled (cf. 1 Kings 2:35).[50]

In all of this, then, we see how the Davidic covenant is not simply a private oath sworn to David. It is the climactic event of the history of God's covenant dealings with mankind in the Old Testament. Through the Davidic king, God will restore the covenant relationship with humanity that was lost since Adam fell at the dawn of time.

---

[50] 1 Chronicles 6:2-12 provides the line of Zadok going back to Phinehas. The line of Abiathar is more difficult to reconstruct. First, we must recognize that there were two men named Phinehas. The first one we shall call Phinehas[1]. Phinehas[1] was the son of Eleazar, the son of Aaron (1 Chron. 6:2). The second Phinehas we shall call Phinehas[2], who was the son of Eli (1 Sam. 14:3). There were also two men with the name "Ahitub." One, Ahitub[1], was the father of Zadok (1 Chron. 6:12); the other, Ahitub[2], was the grandson of Eli (1 Sam. 14:3) and the father of Ahimelech (1 Sam. 22:9), who in turn was the father of Abiathar (1 Sam. 22:20; 23:6). Ahimelech was a descendant of Ithamar—making Abiathar a descendant of Ithamar and not Eleazar/Phinehas (1 Chron. 24:3). While it is possible that Ahimelech's Ithamar descent is on his mother's side, this seems unlikely, since the maternal line is not mentioned.

CHAPTER 3

THEMES OF
THE PSALTER

The Big Picture

The final form of the Psalter dates to the post-exilic era—
that is, the time after the southern kingdom returned from
exile. In this period there was no Davidic king. Indeed, as we
shall see, ten of the twelve tribes were nowhere to be found. It
seemed as though the Davidic covenant had failed. Yet,
because of God's covenant promises, hope remained alive.
After all, God had sworn to David, "your house and your
kingdom shall be made sure for ever before me" (2 Sam. 7:16).
Since the Davidic covenant was not merely a private covenant,
but was linked to the fulfillment of all of God's previously
sworn oaths, the Jewish people were confident that God
would restore the kingdom promised to David. This hope for
the restoration of the Davidic kingdom represents the message
and editorial principle of the Psalter.

Thus, the Psalter is dominated by Davidic themes. Indeed,
most of the psalms are ascribed to David himself. Moreover,
various themes connected to the Davidic covenant recur
throughout the Psalms. These motifs are inextricably linked to
the restoration of the Davidic kingdom. They are as follows:

1. The New Exodus: restoration of the twelve tribes of Israel
   and the nations under the Davidic king
2. Movement from Sinai to Zion

3. The important role of Wisdom and its relationship to the Torah
4. The *Todah*, or "thank offering"[1]

So as to not lose the forest for the trees, it is helpful to look at these elements before beginning an in-depth analysis of the Psalter. A brief treatment of each is necessary because, at first glance, it is difficult to see their connection to the Davidic covenant.

THE NEW EXODUS
Captivating Prophecy

The hope for restoration can be found in germ in the Book of Deuteronomy.[2] Moses entreats Israel to keep the covenant, telling them that if they do they will have life and receive blessing (cf. Deut. 28:1-13). However, failure to keep the covenant would result in the curse of exile to the nations.[3] After issuing these warnings, Moses makes it clear that Israel would in fact fail to keep the covenant and end up in exile, saying: "And when all these things come upon you, *the blessing and the curse . . .*" (Deut. 30:1).

---

[1] There are many other themes in the Book of Psalms, such as "God as refuge" and "divine vengeance," but we cannot examine all of them here.

[2] F.M. Cross posits a post-exilic editor behind the Deuteronomic history who shaped the narrative around the hope of restoration from exile. Cross cites H.W. Wolff, saying he "correctly discerns a theme of hope which comes from the hand of a deuteronomistic editor in the Exile. . . ." F.M. Cross, "The Themes of the Book of Kings and the Structure of the Deuteronomistic History," *Reconsidering Israel and Judah: Recent Studies on the Deuteronomistic History*, Gary Knoppers and J. Gordon McConville, eds. (Winona Lake, IN: Eisenbrauns, 2000), 83. Friedman proposes an exiled priest as the source for Deuteronomy. Richard Friedman, *Who Wrote the Bible?* (New York: Summit Books, 1989), 138.

[3] See Deuteronomy 25:15-68 for the curses of the covenant. It is noteworthy that the Deuteronomic covenant has many more curses than blessings and that it is sworn by Israel through self-maledictory oaths. Hence, Deuteronomy is, in a sense, a lower law. We will discuss this more thoroughly in our analysis of Sinai and Zion. For a treatment of the distinctive characteristics of the Deuteronomic covenant, see Hahn, *Kinship by Covenant*, 108-19.

Now, obviously, this comes as terrible news to Israel. The curse of exile is not only a possible scenario, but an inevitable reality. Yet, Moses promises the people that if they turn to God and repent, He will gather them from the nations to which they have been scattered.

> [T]hen the LORD your God will restore your fortunes, and have compassion upon you, and he will gather you again from all the peoples where the LORD your God has scattered you (Deut. 30:3).

Hence, already in Deuteronomy the hope for restoration is present—even before the exile occurs.

The exile took place in two phases. First, the northern tribes were conquered and scattered by the Assyrian empire in the eighth century B.C. This was preceded by a less ambitious Assyrian program a decade earlier, in which the northern-most tribes of Zebulun and Naphtali were conquered.[4] Two centuries later (586 B.C.), the southern kingdom of Judah was captured and its inhabitants went into captivity in Babylon. However, while the Judeans returned from exile under the reign of the Persian king Cyrus, the northern tribes never returned.[5]

The hope of Israel, then, includes the hope of restoration from exile. One contemporary scholar who has emphasized

---

[4] Later we will further examine the fact that the conquering of northern Israel in 722 B.C. was preceded by an earlier campaign against the northernmost tribes. This will become an important consideration when we discuss Jesus' ministry in Galilee. See Barry Bandstra, *Reading the Old Testament: An Introduction to the Hebrew Bible* (Belmont, CA: Wadsworth Publishing, 1995), 288; and Walter Kaiser, *The Messiah in the Old Testament* (Grand Rapids, MI: Zondervan Publishing House, 1995), 143.

[5] Hence, the question arises as to the fate of the northern tribes, also known as the "lost tribes of Israel." Rabbinic interpretation, for example, is divided on whether or not the ten tribes will return. See Antti Laato, *A Star Is Rising: The Historical Development of the Old Testament Royal Ideology and the Rise of the Jewish Messianic Expectations* (Atlanta: Scholars Press, 1997), 103.

this theme is N.T. Wright, who argues that by the first century the hope of Israel could be equated with the hope of restoration of the kingdom from exile: "The phrase 'kingdom of God,' therefore, carried unambiguously the *hope* that YHWH would act thus, within history, to vindicate Israel."[6]

However, Wright's view of the restoration from exile needs to be nuanced. Wright defines the exile as not only foreign captivity, but extends the meaning to include the occupation and oppression of the Gentile nations. So, even though the southern kingdom returned from exile in 538 B.C., their hopes would not be fully realized until they attained self-rule:

> The great story of the Hebrew scriptures was therefore inevitably read in the second-temple period as a story in search of a conclusion. This ending would have to incorporate the full liberation and redemption of Israel, an event which had not happened as long as Israel was being oppressed, a prisoner in her own land.[7]

The problem with the view that restoration will be complete once the rule of the Davidic monarchy is established is that it ignores the fact that ten of the twelve tribes of Israel remain in exile. Hence, this view does not really reflect the hope for the restoration of the whole kingdom of Israel, but simply that of the kingdom of Judah.

This is related to the common mistake of equating the terms "Israelite" and "Jew." Too often the two terms are used interchangeably. Put simply, while every Jew is an Israelite, not every Israelite is a Jew. "Israelite" denotes a descendant of Jacob/Israel, a member of any of the twelve tribes. A "Jew" is either a member of the tribe of Judah or a resident of the southern

---

[6] N.T. Wright, *Jesus and the Victory of God* (Minneapolis: Fortress Press, 1996), 203.
[7] N.T. Wright, *The New Testament and the People of God* (Minneapolis: Fortress Press, 1992), 217.

region of Judah. Indeed, in the prophetic tradition, it was the northern kingdom that was most commonly called "Israel," while the southern kingdom was simply identified as "Judah."

Support for this distinction between "Israelite" and "Jew" may be found in the fact that, while the Galileans were described as "Israelites," they were not identified necessarily as "Jews." Galilee was formerly part of the northern kingdom. As mentioned before, the Assyrians did not take into captivity the entire population of the northern kingdom in their first campaign. This is clear from the reference to "the remnant of Israel" in 2 Chronicles 34:9.[8] Thus, Galileans, while not designated "Jews," were identified as "Israelites," the descendants of the northern kingdom.[9] So then, the restoration of Israel from exile must include more than simply those of the southern kingdom released from Babylon. The northern tribes must return from their exile as well. This was the message of the Old Testament prophets:

> In that day the Lord will extend his hand yet a second time to recover the remnant which is left of his people, from Assyria, from Egypt, from Pathros, from Ethiopia, from Elam, from Shinar, from Hamath, and from the coastlands of the sea. He will raise an ensign for the nations, and will assemble the outcasts of Israel, and gather the dispersed of Judah from the four corners of the earth. . . . Ephraim shall not be jealous of Judah, and Judah shall not harass Ephraim. . . . And there will be a highway from Assyria for the remnant which is left

---

[8] Richard Horsley, *Archaeology, History and Society in Galilee: The Social Context of Jesus and the Rabbis* (Valley Forge, PA: Trinity Press International, 1996), 23: "Thus, since critical interpretation of Assyrian records clearly suggests that the deportations were mainly of officials and skilled personnel, we must conclude that much of the Israelite population of Galilee must have remained in their villages or perhaps withdrew into the rugged interior. Continuity of the Israelite population into later times therefore seems the most likely conclusion. . . . During the brief interlude between the Assyrian and Babylonian domination, Josiah attempted to reassert Davidic rule over the northern Israelites."

[9] *Ibid.*, 9.

of his people, as there was for Israel when they came up from the land of Egypt" (Is. 11:11-13, 16).

Here we see the distinction between "the outcasts of Israel" and the "dispersed of Judah," between the house of Ephraim and the house of Judah.[10] Other examples of the Pan-Israelite ("pan" meaning *all*) restoration abound throughout the prophets.[11]

This Pan-Israelite hope is also reflected in the writings of the intertestamental period. For example, the Testament of Benjamin states: "The twelve tribes shall be gathered. . . ."[12] Hence, the restoration from exile remained Israel's hope, not only because the southern kingdom was under foreign occupation, but because the ten tribes had not yet been returned. Yet, these ten tribes were so thoroughly scattered to the nations that their return would constitute nothing less than a miracle.[13] Because of this, the scattering of Israel—the "diaspora"—is painted in terms of the death and decomposition of a body, while the restoration of Israel is often described in terms of resurrection from the dead.[14]

---

[10] The northern kingdom was often identified as "Ephraim," since it was first ruled by an Ephraimite king. See 1 Kings 11:26-40.

[11] In fact, it is hard to find a prophet who does not speak of the restoration! See Isaiah 49:5-6; Jeremiah 3:18; Ezekiel 11:16; Hosea 11:10-11; Amos 9:14-15; Micah 4:6-7; and Zechariah 10:8-10. See also Sirach 48:10.

[12] Testament of Benjamin 9:2. See Charlesworth, *Old Testament Pseudepigrapha*, vol. 1, 827.

[13] For a treatment on the rabbinic debate as to whether the ten tribes will return, see A. Neubauer, "Where are the Ten Tribes," *Jewish Quarterly Review*, 1 (1889), 14-28. See also Laato, *A Star Is Rising*, 103. Horsley doesn't even believe such a fulfillment of the prophets is possible. Richard Horsley, *Jesus and the Spiral of Violence: Popular Resistance in Roman Palestine* (San Francisco: Harper and Row Publishers, 1987), 193.

[14] See Ezekiel 37; Hosea 13-14; Daniel 12. Indeed, the word "diaspora" was used most frequently to describe "decomposition." See James M. Scott, "Exile and the Self-Understanding of Diaspora Jews," *Exile: Old Testament, Jewish and Christian Conceptions*, James M. Scott, ed. (Leiden, The Netherlands: Brill, 1997), 178-79.

Still in the Wilderness

However, the dominant image used by the prophets to describe the hope for the restoration from exile is Exodus imagery, deeming the return of the captives as the "New Exodus." This is the dominant theme of Isaiah 40-55. Rikki Watts explains:

> Although other canonical writings appeal to the Exodus tradition, here it is elevated to its most prominent status as a hermeneutic, and according to some commentators, shapes the heart of 40-55.[15]

Examples of Exodus imagery that refer to the New Exodus include wilderness imagery, the theme of "the way," sea imagery, and references to "sing a new song to the Lord." These themes are especially brought out in Book IV of the Psalter.

Yet, the New Exodus is greater than the first Exodus. The second will bring about the conversion of the nations who will come with Israel to Zion, whereas in the first, only Israel was delivered and established in the Promised Land. The prophet Micah writes:

> [M]any nations shall come, and say: "Come, let us go up to the mountain of the LORD, to the house of the God of Jacob; that he may teach us his ways and we may walk in his paths." For out of Zion shall go forth the law, and the word of the LORD from Jerusalem (Mic. 4:2).

Similarly, in Isaiah we read:

> It is too light a thing that you should be my servant to raise up the tribes of Jacob and to restore the preserved of Israel; I will give you as a light to the nations, that my salvation may reach to the end of the earth (Is. 49:6).

---

[15] Rikki E. Watts, *Isaiah's New Exodus and Mark* (Tübingen: J.C.B. Mohr, 1997), 79.

Thus, the Lord's restoration of His people will convince the nations that He is the true God, and they will turn to Him (see e.g., Ezek. 36:23-24).

Finally, the New Exodus cannot be separated from the Davidic covenant. Just as it was David who first united Israel, so too, the gathering of Israel from the nations would happen under the Davidic king.[16] Further, this restored Davidic kingdom included an international vision.

The restoration of the Davidic kingdom and the New Exodus are linked. In Jeremiah 23, the New Exodus follows the Lord's promise that He will raise up for David a righteous branch who shall reign as king. Likewise, Amos promises that Israel will be restored, but only after the return of the Davidic king: "In that day I will raise up the booth of David that is fallen . . ." (Amos 9:11).

The Psalter is full of imagery of the New Exodus. For example, Psalm 137 describes Israel's captivity in Babylon:

> By the waters of Babylon, there we sat down and wept, when we remembered Zion. . . . For there our captors required of us songs . . . saying, "Sing us one of the songs of Zion!" (137:1, 3).

Psalm 120 states: "Woe is me, that I sojourn in Meshech, that I dwell among the tents of Kedar! Too long have I had my dwelling among those who hate peace" (120:5-6). Psalm 106:47 reads, "gather us from among the nations" and Psalm 147:2 explains that the Lord "gathers the outcasts of Israel." Hence, the Psalms frequently cry out to God asking Him to "restore" His people.

---

[16] See Laato, *A Star Is Rising*, 176.

FROM SINAI TO ZION
Moving on Up

There is a clear movement from Sinai to Zion represented by the Davidic covenant. Sinai represents the Mosaic tradition, a national covenant, especially linked with ceremonial laws. Zion, however, represents an international arrangement.

Zion was taken by David in 2 Samuel 5. It soon became the home of the Davidic palace and, thus, Zion became identified with the Davidic king.[17] Indeed, scholars such as Gese tell us that Zion was understood to be the property of the Davidic king. Quite naturally, Zion came to be known as "the city of David" (2 Sam. 5:7).

The Temple is also identified with Mount Zion: "May he send you help from the sanctuary, and give you support from Zion" (Ps. 20:3). Likewise, Psalm 134 speaks of the priests who serve "in the house of the LORD" (v. 1) and instructs them to "lift up your hands to the holy place" (v. 2) so that God may bless them "from Zion" (v. 3).

Yet, there remains another possible reason why God's house was equated with Zion. Before the Temple was built, there were two principal cultic sites. First, there was the tent built in the wilderness under Moses, which was at Gibeon. Here sacrifices were offered continually according to the Law (cf. 1 Chron. 16:39-40). At the same time, there was another tent pitched by David, located in Zion, where only *todah* or thank offerings were made (cf. 1 Chron. 16:1-6).

In the Zion tent, David sang the first *todah*. In fact, the song David sings is recorded in 1 Chronicles 16:8-34. This song later appears as Psalm 96, but with one very interesting addition. Whereas 1 Chronicles 16:29 says, "bring an offering,

---

[17] Cf. Richard Hess and Gordon Wenham, *Zion: City of Our God* (Grand Rapids, MI: William B. Eerdmans Publishing, 1999), 2-3; Hartmut Gese, *Essays on Biblical Theology* (Minneapolis: Augsburg Publishing House, 1981), 26: "Zion . . . belonged to David's family."

and come before him!" Psalm 96:8 adds, "come into his courts!" The reference to the Lord's "courts" clearly refers to the Temple. Here we can see how a psalm originally sung by David at the Zion tent was later adopted for Temple use.[18]

In the building of the Temple by Solomon, the son of David, we see the further fulfillment of the Abrahamic covenant. The place where Abraham offered Isaac is Mount Moriah, the same mountain range where the later Temple stands.[19] Instead of offering Isaac, Abraham offered a ram as a substitute sacrifice. It was there that God promised to bless all nations. Hence, the Temple cult is a reminder to God of the covenant oath He swore to save all mankind.[20]

The construction of the Temple also represents continuity with the Deuteronomic covenant. As we saw earlier, David realized that by conquering the final Jebusite stronghold of Zion, he had thereby gained rest from his enemies and thus had fulfilled the conditions of Deuteronomy 12 for the establishment of God's permanent dwelling place. Hence, the Temple itself is a visible sign of the Davidic covenant's fulfillment of the Abrahamic and Deuteronomic covenants.

Moreover, the sacrifices of the Temple may also represent God's judgment of the gods of the nations who have taken Israel captive. An example of this is Psalm 68, which speaks of going to God's "sanctuary" (v. 24). Immediately following the description of foreign kings bearing gifts in the Temple, the psalm condemns the animals worshipped as gods by these pagan peoples. "Because of thy temple at Jerusalem kings bear gifts to thee. Rebuke the beasts that dwell among the reeds, the herd of bulls with the calves of the peoples" (vv. 29-30).

---

[18] Evidence for this distinction between the Temple and the "tent" may be found in the Septuagint. In Psalm 28, the superscription tells us that the psalm was sung for the dedication of the tent.
[19] Cf. Levenson, *Sinai and Zion*, 94.
[20] Cf. Hahn, *Kinship by Covenant*, 347.

Israel itself had fallen into the worship of "bulls" and "calves" and was, therefore, ordered to sacrifice them to renounce their idolatry. Hence, in the Temple the restoration, celebrated as God's judgment on pagan gods, is ritually enacted.[21]

Because of its connection with the Abrahamic covenant, Zion represents the hope of the unification of all nations under Yahweh. This international element is the most distinctive characteristic of the move from Sinai to Zion. Zion's international dimension stands in stark contrast to Sinai, where God quarantined Israel from the nations. While the Sinai covenant represented a national covenant, Zion represents an international covenant.[22] Stuhlmacher explains: "The torah that goes from Zion no longer applies to Israel alone, nor separates them, the people of God, from the Gentiles, but is directed to all nations."[23]

Widening the Tent Pegs

The movement from the national to the international is manifested in the replacement of the tent with the Temple. With the building of the Temple by the son of David, the Gentiles finally have a fitting place to worship the God of Israel. Hence, the Temple of Solomon, and the later Jerusalem Temples in imitation of it, included the Court of the Gentiles. Underscoring this international quality of the Temple,

[21] Cf. Cristiano Grottanelli, *Kings and Prophets: Monarchic Power, Inspired Leadership, and Sacred Text in Biblical Narrative* (New York: Oxford University Press, 1999), 47-69.

[22] Gese explains that on Sinai God only revealed Himself to Israel, whereas on Zion He reveals Himself to the nations. See Gese, *Essays in Biblical Theology*, 26. See also Hess and Wenham, who understand Zion as representing the military strength of the Davidic kingdom—which is understood as manifesting God's dominion over all the nations (Hess and Wenham, *Zion*, 6); and Walter Kaiser, *The Messiah in the Old Testament* (Grand Rapids, MI: Zondervan Publishing House, 1995), 80: "[W]hat David received is to be conveyed to everyone including all the Gentiles and nations of the earth."

[23] Peter Stuhlmacher, *Reconciliation, Law & Righteousness: Essays in Biblical Theology* (Philadelphia: Fortress Press, 1986), 115. Cf. Ps. 102:16-17; Is. 2:2-3.

Scripture tells us that a Gentile even assisted in the building process (1 Kings 5).

However, despite the international aspect of Zion, it must be noted that Zion also remains a place where *all Israel*—that is, all twelve tribes—is gathered together.[24] Zion represents the Davidic kingdom that, in its golden age, united all twelve tribes of Israel. Thus, after the exile, Zion represents the place where all Israel will be reunited: "And the ransomed of the LORD shall return, and come to Zion with singing; . . ." (Is. 51:11). Isaiah goes on to say: "For as soon as Zion was in labor she brought forth her sons" (Is. 66:8).

Likewise, when Israel is restored God will also bring the nations to Himself on Mount Zion. Isaiah 2:2 states that "all the nations shall flow to [Zion]." Further, from Zion God's law will go out to teach the nations His ways: "For out of Zion shall go forth the law, and the word of the LORD from Jerusalem" (Is. 2:3).

In summary, then, Zion represents both the reunification of Israel and of all the nations. Zion represents the great accomplishment of the Davidic rule—a Pan-Israelite kingdom that includes the nations. Hence, the hope for the restoration of the kingdom is inextricably bound to Zion.[25]

Zion is a recurring theme throughout the Psalms. From the beginning of the Psalter, it is understood as the place of the throne of David: "I have set my king on Zion, my holy hill" (Ps. 2:6). Likewise, Psalm 132:17 states of Zion: "There I will make a horn to sprout for David."

Even more, Zion is associated with the place where God reigns as King from His Temple: "O LORD, who shall sojourn

---

[24] See Hess and Wenham, *Zion*, 2.
[25] Ben Halpern, "Zion in Modern Literature: II. Hebrew Prose," *Zion in Jewish Literature*, Abraham S. Halkin, ed. (Lenham, MD: University Press of America, 1988), 121: "Exile is the problem for which Zion is the solution, as Zion is the future goal towards which Exile is the present path."

in thy tent? Who shall dwell on thy holy hill?" (Ps. 15:1). Zion is the source of divine assistance: "May he send you help from the sanctuary, and give you support from Zion!" (Ps. 20:2). Zion is also the location of God's throne: "The LORD reigns; let the peoples tremble! He sits enthroned upon the cherubim; . . . The LORD is great in Zion" (Ps. 99:1-2).

Deliverance is also depicted as coming from Zion, as in Psalm 20:2: "May he send you help from the sanctuary, and give you support from Zion!" From Zion God calls out to the earth: "Out of Zion, the perfection of beauty, God shines forth" (Ps. 50:2); and from Zion He answers the prayers of His people: "I cry aloud to the LORD, and he answers me from his holy hill" (Ps. 3:4).

The restoration is intimately connected with Zion: "O that deliverance for Israel would come out of Zion! When the LORD restores the fortunes of his people, Jacob shall rejoice, Israel shall be glad" (Ps. 14:7). As in Isaiah, Zion gives birth to children, for it is there that the nations will come to worship the Lord: "And of Zion it shall be said, 'This one and that one were born in her'. . . The LORD records as he registers the peoples, 'This one was born there'" (Ps. 87:5-6).

The most important song relating to Zion, though, is probably Psalm 68. There the movement from Sinai to Zion is explicitly described: "[T]he Lord came from Sinai into the holy place" (v. 17). The coming of the Lord to the holy mountain is also associated with the return of the captives: "I will bring them back from Bashan, I will bring them back from the depths of the sea" (v. 22). The northern and southern tribes are united there: "There is Benjamin, the least of them, in the lead, the princes of Judah in their throng, the princes of Zebulun, the princes of Naphtali" (v. 27). Zion is also linked with the turning of the nations to worship the Lord: "[L]et Ethiopia hasten to stretch out her hands to God. Sing to God, O kingdoms of the earth; sing praises to the Lord" (vv. 31-32).

WISDOM LITERATURE:
TORAH FOR THE DAVIDIC COVENANT
Law Abiding

Closely associated with the Davidic covenant is the Wisdom literature. The Wisdom literature includes Job, Proverbs, Ecclesiastes, the Song of Solomon, Wisdom, and Sirach.[26] Of these, Proverbs, Ecclesiastes, the Song of Solomon, and Wisdom are all attributed to Solomon. Since it is beyond the scope of this study to examine these books individually, a few general remarks about the Wisdom literature will suffice.

The Wisdom literature reflects the international quality of the Davidic covenant. It does not concern itself with the ritual laws of Sinai given exclusively to Israel; rather, it addresses anyone who seeks righteousness.[27] This is especially evident in the Book of Job. There we read about how Job, a Gentile, is declared righteous and goes on to mediate for his fellow man through prayer and sacrifice (cf. Job 42:7-8).

Wisdom is also associated with the move from Sinai to Zion. In Sirach 24:4, Wisdom is identified as the "pillar of cloud" which accompanied Israel in the desert. In addition, Wisdom's seeking a place of "rest" in 24:7 has strong connections to Numbers 10:33 and Deuteronomy 1:33, both of which chronicle Israel's similar quest in its desert wanderings.[28] Yet, in Sirach 24:8, Wisdom tells how she finally came to dwell in the central sanctuary in Zion, fulfilling the prophecy

---

[26] Protestants omit Wisdom and Sirach from their canon. The historical reason for this is that Martin Luther resurrected Jerome's concern that since there were no extant Hebrew originals for these books, they may have been forged. However, this argument against their canonicity is no longer valid, since manuscripts of Sirach in Hebrew were found in the Dead Sea collection.

[27] Leo Perdue, *Wisdom & Creation* (Nashville, TN: Abingdon Press, 1994), 87: "Wisdom invites people to pursue their course of study with her and to take up the path of the moral life that she offers. . . . This is a universal call to all who would learn from her."

[28] Gerald Sheppard, *Wisdom as a Hermeneutical Construct* (New York: Walter de Gruyter, 1980), 39.

of Deuteronomy 12. The Davidic connection with Wisdom in light of this move is clear, since the establishment of Zion is identified with the Davidic kingdom.[29]

Therefore, David's fulfillment of the conditions of Deuteronomy is identified as the reception of Wisdom. Deuteronomy 4 states that keeping the law will be Israel's "wisdom" and fulfilling the law will make Israel a "wise" nation (cf. Deut. 4:6-7). Sirach 24 portrays the fulfillment of the Deuteronomic covenant in terms of Israel's reception of wisdom. Indeed, part of Moses' final address is quoted verbatim in Sirach 24:23. It seems, then, that Sirach 24 is showing Israel that wisdom has never been far from them—echoing the words of Moses in Deuteronomy 32.[30] However, the attainment of wisdom has only come about with the dawning of the Davidic covenant, which also marks the fulfillment of the Deuteronomic covenant. In other words, the Davidic covenant fulfills Deuteronomy through its reception of wisdom.

Moreover, other ancient Near East cultures had similar literature. The Egyptians, for example, had their own set of moral proverbs. Hence, the Wisdom literature may be understood as Israel's attempt to accommodate the teaching of Yahweh to the nations by dropping distinctive elements of Israelite tradition, especially cultic law, and deliberately harnessing modes of communication already used by the nations. "The absence of these traditions is further underscored by the international character of wisdom."[31]

---

[29] Sheppard thus shows how Sirach 24 recalls 2 Samuel 6-7. See *ibid.*, 49.

[30] *Ibid.*, 66: "[If] one reads Deut. 4 and 32 together alongside of Deut. 30, the conception emerges of a *book of Torah* (ch. 30) which comes near to Israel (chapters 4 and 30) from beyond the heavens and is her *wisdom* (chapters 4 and 32). This imagery coincides perfectly with the presuppositions of Sirach 24:23" (original emphasis).

[31] Roland Murphy and Elizabeth Huwiler, *Proverbs, Ecclesiastes, Song of Songs* (Peabody, MA: Hendrickson Publishers, 1999), 3.

Further, Wisdom is presented in terms of priestly ministry: "In the holy tabernacle I ministered before him" (Sir. 24:10).[32] In a sense, then, we see that the fulfillment of the Deuteronomic covenant implies priestly service. That's why David became a priest-king upon fulfilling the conditions of Deuteronomy. Wisdom is meant, therefore, to restore priesthood. This may be understood as the significance of the *Todah*, in which an individual offers thanksgiving in the midst of suffering—making his prayer his sacrifice.

The Davidic covenant completes the international vision that the lower law of Deuteronomy was meant to achieve through Israel. Hence through the Davidic covenant, God brings His law to the nations, not through an exclusive Israelite ritual law code, but through the universality of the Wisdom literature. Since this partially reverses the effects of Adam's fall, it should be no surprise that wisdom is often linked with Edenic imagery.[33]

There is also a discernible progression of understanding through the Solomonic wisdom collection. In Proverbs, Solomon teaches that if a man is righteous, he will be rewarded with a happy life and earthly blessings. In Ecclesiastes, however, Solomon realizes that earthly prosperity is vanity. This leads to a kind of cynicism. In the Song of Songs, the king turns his attention to seeking out his beloved, who is later identified as Lady Wisdom in the Book of Wisdom: "I loved her and sought her from my youth, and I desired to take her for my bride, and I became enamored of her beauty" (Wis. 8:2). Finally, the Book of Wisdom elevates wisdom to the status of divinity (cf. Wis. 7:25-26). Hence, Solomon learns that one

---

[32] Sheppard, *Wisdom as a Hermeneutical Construct*, 48.
[33] For example, wisdom is called the "tree of life" (Prov. 3:18). For a treatment of the Edenic imagery used to describe wisdom in Sirach, see *ibid.*, 101-02. See also Perdue, *Wisdom & Creation*, 271.

does not seek wisdom for the sake of receiving blessing, but for the sake of communion with God.

In this vein, the Book of Wisdom exhibits a deeper understanding than does Proverbs. Proverbs taught that the righteous man will be rewarded with a happy life on earth. By the time of the Book of Wisdom, Solomon has learned that this is not man's ultimate goal. The true reward for the righteous is not necessarily realized on earth, but in the afterlife:

> In the eyes of the foolish they seemed to have died, and their departure was thought to be an affliction, and their going from us to be their destruction; but they are at peace (Wis. 3:2-3).

Hence, the righteous *will* suffer on earth in order to receive a greater good—God Himself:

> Having been disciplined a little, they will receive great good, because God tested them and found them worthy of himself; like gold in the furnace he tried them, and like a sacrificial burnt offering he accepted them (Wis. 3:5-6).

The truth Adam failed to realize is finally understood by the Davidic king.

If the Mosaic Torah, which was meant to make Israel a light to the nations, is identified with Sinai, the Wisdom literature should be identified as the Torah of the Davidic covenant that comes forth from Zion. Support for this claim can be found in 2 Samuel 7:19, where, upon receiving God's sworn covenant oath to establish his dynasty, David declares: "You have shown me a *torah for mankind*." This is the law that goes forth from Zion, in Isaiah 2:3. This *torah for mankind,* the *torah for adam,* is the Wisdom literature.[34]

---

[34] Hahn, *A Father Who Keeps His Promises*, 213: "The 'torah' came to the Gentiles initially through Solomon, in the form of God's 'wisdom' (see 1 Kings 3-10), and was subsequently collected and associated with what we call the Wisdom Literature."

THE *TODAH* OFFERING
How David Gave Himself Todah-ly

The Psalter also represents a shift in emphasis from the *hattat*, that is, the "sin offering," to the "thank offering," known as the *todah*. Leviticus 7:12 *et seq.* specifically provides for this unique sacrifice. The *todah* is closely linked with an *ordeal* involving some kind of suffering or threat. Let us look at this more closely.

The *todah* is the only sacrifice in which bread is offered as sacrifice.[35] The sacrifice was then eaten in a celebratory meal.[36] This is also the only time the Levitical law code permitted consecrated bread to be eaten by lay Israelites. However, while this sacrifice is found in the Mosaic law, like the concept of wisdom, it is not fully developed until the time of David.

Though the *todah* is found in Scripture before him, David brought the *todah* sacrifice to the forefront of Israel's cultic life. The Book of Psalms, largely attributed to Davidic traditions, is the most plentiful source for understanding the *todah* offering. Moreover, in the tent established by David on Zion, the priests were appointed in order to offer *todah* offerings, not sin offerings (cf. 1 Chron. 16:4, 7). David himself dedicates the tent with a *todah* song of his own (cf. 1 Chron. 16:7-37). Hence, the *todah* offering is uniquely related to the Davidic kingdom.

A *todah* sacrifice begins in the midst of the experience of suffering or oppression. When an Israelite finds himself in a life-threatening dilemma, he begins his *todah* with a prayer for deliverance. Once deliverance occurs, a meal is held in which the one delivered recounts the Lord's merciful intervention.[37]

---

[35] Gese, *Essays on Biblical Theology*, 130: "In contrast to the meal offering, the thank offering includes not only a bloody offering of meat, but a bloodless offering of bread, and it is the only sacrifice that includes leavened bread."

[36] Drijvers, *The Psalms, Their Structure and Meaning*, 83.

[37] Gese, *Essays on Biblical Theology*, 81.

The *todah* is, therefore, closely linked to the proclamation of God's saving deeds.[38]

The prayer for deliverance is accompanied by a vow to offer a sacrifice once the distressed petitioner is rescued:

> I will come into thy house with burnt offerings; I will pay thee my vows, that which my lips uttered and my mouth promised when I was in trouble. I will offer to thee burnt offerings of fatlings, with the smoke of the sacrifice of rams; I will make an offering of bulls and goats (Ps. 66:13-15; cf. 56:12).

By offering up his sacrifice, the supplicant completes his "vow" to the Lord.

One interesting point concerning the *todah* is this: It is not clear whether the act of thanksgiving occurs before or after deliverance.[39] The singer of the *todah* often proclaims thanksgiving in anticipation, proclaiming that the Lord has already "answered me" or that He has "heard my supplications." Other times it seems that the prayer of thanksgiving is offered following deliverance (cf. Ps. 69:30). Therefore, we cannot be sure whether the act of thanksgiving had a fixed place before or after the ordeal.

Psalm 50 is a clear example of a *todah* offered prior to deliverance:

> Offer to God a sacrifice of thanksgiving, and pay your vows to the Most High; and call upon me in the day of trouble; I will deliver you, and you shall glorify me (vv. 14-15).

---

[38] Harvey Guthrie, *Theology As Thanksgiving: From Israel's Psalms to the Church's Eucharist* (New York: Seabury Press, 1981), 79: "Above all else, the *todah* cult is a cult of remembering, of calling to mind, of living again events which have occurred where the human community could see and experience and appropriate them as its own."

[39] Psalm 26:7, for example, appears to indicate that the deliverance has already taken place, but the request of v. 9 and the future act of blessing the Lord in v. 12 seem to indicate that the singer of the *todah* remains afflicted.

Here God says offer thanksgiving and call upon me, *then* I will deliver you.

Another example of this is Psalm 9. The psalm begins with an act of *todah*, which seems to celebrate the definitive vanquishing of the psalmist's enemies:

> When my enemies turned back, they stumbled and perished before thee. . . . Thou hast rebuked the nations, thou hast destroyed the wicked; thou hast blotted out their name for ever and ever. The enemy have vanished in everlasting ruins; their cities thou hast rooted out; the very memory of them has perished (Ps. 9:3, 5-6).

However, the psalmist ends by saying that the wicked "shall depart," petitioning the Lord to stop the nations from prevailing: "The wicked shall depart to Sheol. . . . Arise, O LORD! Let not man prevail; let the nations be judged before thee!" (Ps. 9:17, 19). This indicates that final deliverance has not yet occurred.

Praying for Deliverance

It is clear that the declaration of thanksgiving and the accompanying *todah* sacrifice are inextricably linked with the experience of suffering. The *todah*, then, represents the sacrifice not only of the slaughtered animal, but also of the person, who offers up his suffering as a sacrifice, trusting in the Lord to deliver him.[40] This is evident in Psalm 69:

> I will praise the name of God with a song; I will magnify him with thanksgiving. This will please the LORD more than an ox or a bull with horns and hoofs. Let the oppressed see it and be glad (vv. 30-32).

---

[40] Gese, *Essays on Biblical Theology*, 132: "In these psalms we do not have the expression of an enlightened critique of sacrifice, but rather the total involvement of the person in the essence of sacrifice, as that involvement grew out of a deeply rooted spiritual understanding of the thank offering."

In this psalm David is teaching the persecuted that their suffering counts as a sacrifice to the Lord, so long as it is done with a trusting heart that magnifies itself in thanksgiving.[41]

At the same time, the element of deliverance should not be forgotten. The *todah* psalms are principally requests to be delivered from suffering. Deliverance is not understood as the alternative to the self-offering of the individual, but as the acceptance of his sacrifice, since it reveals that the Lord has truly heard his prayer.[42]

The *todah*, therefore, like the Wisdom literature, represents the internalization and, thus, the fulfillment of the Deuteronomic covenant. The self-offering Adam refused is accomplished in this sacrifice. This is another way the Davidic covenant fulfills the conditions of previous covenants.

Because of its link to the Davidic covenant, the *todah* is bound up with the hope of the restoration of the kingdom. Hence, Gese sees Isaiah 25 as depicting the eschatological feast as one corporate *todah* celebration, in which Israel, delivered from its ordeal of exile, reunites to thank God. Gese goes on to quote an ancient tradition which stated that when the new age comes, that is, when the Davidic kingdom is restored, "all sacrifices will cease, but the thank offering will never cease."[43]

---

[41] The idea that the sacrifice of the animal is secondary and that sacrifice of self is what really counts is especially clear from the penitential Psalms. In Psalm 51, David shows that sacrifice of animals is only acceptable after one sacrifices oneself in the form of a broken spirit (Ps. 51:16-17, 19). See also Psalms 40:6-8; 110:3; 116:6; and 141:2.

[42] The harmony of deliverance and self-sacrifice is also especially clear in the penitential psalms. There, deliverance is redemption from sin, which comes about through one's internal sacrifice: "The deliverance that God is asked to grant is the forgiveness of sin, and new spiritual relationship to God, and in addition the external sacrifice of thanksgiving is transformed into an inward sacrifice of one's own life." Gese, *Essays on Biblical Theology*, 132.

[43] *Ibid.*, 133: "Just as Psalms of thanks can express the spirit of apocalypticism, so the apocalyptic texts can display the spirituality of the thanksgiving sacrifice. At the eschatological feast of the kingdom, Isaiah 25:1-10a, which corresponds to

One final word about *todah* psalms. Since *todah* both referred to a particular type of offering and also can simply mean "thanksgiving," it is difficult to classify a psalm as necessarily referring to a *todah offering*. There are some psalms of "thanksgiving" that are not *todah* psalms.[44] At the same time, other psalms seem to be clearly part of a *todah*, although the word "thanksgiving" is never used.[45]

Thus, there is much gray area when it comes to classifying specific psalms as *todah* psalms. Indeed, the one and only psalm that is explicitly labeled as "A Psalm for the thank offering," Psalm 100, makes no account of a sacrifice, an ordeal, or any retelling of deliverance. Even so, the *todah* is clearly the principal cult of the Book of Psalms.[46] Thus, the *todah* always remains in the backdrop of the Psalter regardless of which individual psalms may be labeled as such. It is necessary to keep this in mind as we now open the Psalter.

---

the feast of the Sinai covenant, Exodus 24 (cf. Is. 24:23c; Ex. 24:9-11), but is celebrated on Mount Zion with all the nations, the song of thanksgiving is sung (vv. 1-4) and this transforms the feast into the thank offering of the entire spiritual community of God."

[44] Psalm 136, for example, is a kind of corporate thanksgiving, but since the *todah* was a sacrifice offered by an individual, Psalm 136 cannot be classified as a *todah* psalm.

[45] For example, Psalm 66 contains the prayer of an individual who comes before the Lord with a sacrifice, recounting his deliverance, paying his vows, and making the offering he "promised when [he] was in trouble" (v. 14), which he promised to offer once delivered from his affliction.

[46] Indeed, sin offerings are often condemned as insufficient in the Psalter (e.g., Ps. 40:6; 50:8-9; 51:16; and 69:30-31).

CHAPTER 4

A CANONICAL STUDY OF THE BOOK OF PSALMS

Now that we have identified some recurring themes in the Psalter, it is time to see how the organization of the Psalms underscores Israel's hope for the restoration of the kingdom from exile. It is important to note that many of the psalms had already been written before being placed into the final form of the Psalter.[1] For this reason, the organization of the psalms is often very subtle and requires close examination.

While the individual psalms themselves may be very early in origin, the final organization of the Psalter into 150 psalms must be placed sometime in the late post-exilic period. In fact, the earliest evidence we have of the canonical form of the Psalter is the Septuagint (LXX), which dates to the early part of the second century B.C.[2] The Masoretic Psalter (MT), in its final form, cannot be dated until sometime later.[3] Elements of

---

[1] This is evidenced by the many psalms whose texts are found in 1 Chronicles, which predates the final form of the Psalter. Such psalms are Psalm 96:1-13 = 1 Chronicles 16:23-33; Psalm 105:1-15 = 1 Chronicles 16:18-22; Psalm 106:1 = 1 Chronicles 16:34; and Psalm 106:35-36 = 1 Chronicles 16:35-36.

[2] David Mitchell, *The Message of the Psalter* (Sheffield, England: Sheffield Press, 1997), 16.

[3] The Masoretic text is the product of Jewish redaction and was profoundly influenced by the destruction of the Temple in 70 A.D. and the rise of Christianity. See Gese, *Essay on Biblical Theology*, 30. This is also evidenced by the work of F.M. Cross, who, upon analyzing the copies of biblical books found at Qumran, found that they had more in common with the LXX than the Masoretic text. See Hershel Shanks, *Frank Moore Cross: Conversations with a Bible Scholar* (Washington: Biblical Archaeology Society, 1994), 123.

the eschatological hopes found in the Greek Psalter were omitted from the Masoretic text, reflecting the impact of the destruction of Jerusalem in 70 A.D.[4]

However, despite minor variations, it is clear that the MT and the LXX contain the same psalms, placed in the same order, though their numbering is slightly different.[5] The New Testament authors seem to have been aware of the LXX/MT arrangement of the psalms. Saint Paul, for example, quotes Psalm 2, referring to it as the "second psalm" (Acts 13:33).

The Qumran scrolls also provide useful information for our study of the Psalter. The Qumran community closely followed the arrangement of the psalms in Books I-III (1-89) of the LXX/MT Psalter. However, the psalms of Books IV-V (90-150) seem to be organized in a completely different manner. In fact, interspersed throughout these later psalms are apocryphal works. For this reason, many scholars question whether this departure from the canonical form of the Psalter is the result of a deliberate editorial intent, or whether the arrangement of the final two books of the Psalter had not yet received acceptance.[6]

However, this question wrongly assumes that a canon is not the product of editorial intent. Indeed, it is clear that there was a certain editorial intent at work in arranging the psalms

---

[4] The majority of superscriptions in Book I of the LXX read: (εἰς τὸ τέλος), or "for the end." Likewise, many of the psalms speak of resurrection (e.g., Ps. 1:5). See Joachim Schaper, *Eschatology in the Greek Psalter* (Tübingen, Germany: J.C.B. Mohr, 1995), 47.

[5] The LXX combines MT Psalms 9-10 and 114-15, while it separates MT Psalms 116 and 147 into two. See Mitchell, *The Message of the Psalter*, 16.

[6] Sanders believes that Qumran gives us a peek into an earlier stage of the development of the canonical Psalter. See James Sanders, *The Dead Sea Psalms Scroll* (Ithaca, NY: Cornell University Press, 1967), 9-10. Patrick W. Skehan believes that the psalms at Qumran were intentionally organized in a way contrary to the LXX/MT Psalter, thus arguing that no question of conflict emerges between the Qumran arrangements and the final LXX/MT form. For a treatment of this debate, see Wilson, *The Editing of the Hebrew Psalter*, 62-92.

in the Dead Sea collection.[7] Nevertheless, it is impossible to argue from the Qumran scrolls that an alternative, authoritative Psalter was used by the community there, since there are many inconsistencies in their own psalm material.[8]

The Five Books of David

In addition to the arrangement of 150 psalms, the Psalter is divided up into five books, as already alluded to above: I = 1-41; II = 42-72, III = 73-89; IV = 90-106; and V = 107-150 (see chart on next page). This seems to evoke the Mosaic Torah, the five books of Moses. But how? Some scholars have even opined that the 150 psalms were part of a triennial lectionary cycle.[9] Yet, while one cannot completely ignore the implied relationship with the Torah, the Mosaic allusion is of secondary importance. What is of primary importance is the way the five books are actually divided. Books I-III are organized around Davidic royal psalms, which function as "seams."[10] Books IV-V seem to have a different organizational pattern, revolving around psalms of *hllwyh-hwdw*.[11] These psalms of "praise" and "thanks" are responses to the restoration of the kingdom and the New Exodus.

---

[7] The psalm collections of Qumran tend to highlight the role of the Davidic king. First, there is the omission of Yahweh kingship psalms, which are primarily found in Book IV. Second, there is the insertion of Davidic literature into the psalm collections. These include portions of canonical books, such as 2 Samuel, as well as apocryphal books. See Gerald Wilson, "The Qumran *Psalms Scroll* (11QPsᵃ) and the Canonical Psalter: Comparison of Editorial Shaping," *Catholic Biblical Quarterly*, 59 (July 1997): 453-54.

[8] Wilson, *The Editing of the Hebrew Psalter*, 69: "[I]t is not possible to demonstrate the existence of a single consistent Psalter tradition at Qumran."

[9] See E.G. King, "The Influence of the Triennial Cycle upon the Psalter," *Journal of Theological Studies*, 5 (1903): 203-13. See also Aileen Guilding, "Some Obscured Rubrics and Lectionary Allusions in the Psalter," *Journal of Theological Studies*, 3 (1952): 41-55; Mitchell, *The Message of the Psalter*, 53-54.

[10] Gerald Wilson, "The Use of Royal Psalms at the 'Seams' of the Hebrew Psalter," *Journal for the Study of the Old Testament*, 35 (1986): 87-88.

[11] Gerald Wilson, "Evidence of Editorial Divisions in the Hebrew Psalter," *Vetus Testamentum*, 3 (1984): 349-52.

Book I is actually one complete collection of Davidic psalms.[12] Psalm 41, while not exhibiting royal characteristics *per se*, ends this first "collection of the king."[13] It concludes with a benediction: "Blessed be the Lord, the God of Israel, from everlasting to everlasting! Amen and Amen" (Ps. 41:13).

The second Book ends with Psalm 72. The superscription reads, "A Psalm of Solomon." However, since the psalm ends with a postscript, "The prayers of David, the son of Jesse, are ended," it may be best to understand this as a psalm "for" Solomon sung by David.[14] The psalm is a celebration of the worldwide dominion of the Davidic kingdom and also ends with a benediction concluding, as Psalm 41 did, with a double "Amen" (cf. Ps. 72:18-19).

Next, there is Psalm 89, which concludes Book III. Psalm 89 is not sung by David but by Ethan, an Ezrahite. Nonetheless, its Davidic kingship stamp is clear. In fact, Psalm 89 contains the most comprehensive declaration of the Davidic covenant in the entire Psalter, lasting fifty-two verses. This psalm marks the boundary between Books III and IV, ending as the other "seam" psalms do with a double "Amen" (cf. Ps. 89:52).

Just as the Davidic kingdom is central to the first Book, a similar argument may be made for Books II and III. Though

---

[12] All of the superscriptions in Book I attribute the psalms to David. In the LXX every psalm has a Davidic superscription. However, in the MT, Psalms 10 and 33 have no heading at all. It should be noted that in the LXX, Psalm 10 (in the MT), is part of the previous psalm, while the LXX version of MT 33 is ascribed to David. Wilson argues that a psalm with no superscription is meant to indicate its link with the psalm prior to it: "In the first three books of the Psalter there are only four psalms which are completely 'untitled' (x, xxxiiii, xliii and lxxi). For each of these there is strong manuscript tradition for combination with the immediately preceding psalm" (*ibid.*, 338).

[13] See Wilson, "The Use of the Royal Psalms," 87.

[14] Cole, *The Shape and Message of Book III*, 182: "Psalm 72 is the culmination of David's prayers, according to the final verse (20) of its doxology . . . thereby interpreting the superscription as 'for,' not 'by' Solomon."

these books contain many psalms attributed to the priestly clans of Asaph and Korah, it is evident that the second Davidic collection (51-72) is meant to be the center. Here there seems to be a deliberate structure, highlighting the Davidic psalms:

```
Korah   42-49
 Asaph   50
  David   51-72
 Asaph   73-83
Korah   84-87[15]
```

Thus the two Levitical collections are intended to function as bookends for the second Davidic collection.[16] This arrangement exhibits clear editorial intent in not only the combination of Books II and III, separated by Davidic Psalm 72, but also in the psalms found within them.[17]

There is a definite movement, though subtle, through these three books that reveals a certain editorial shaping. Although we will sketch this out more carefully as we move through the Psalter, a bird's-eye view would go something like this:

Book I is clearly dominated by David and seems to end with his death. Books II-III, then, portray the fall of the kingdom and the taking of Israel into exile. This climaxes in Psalm 89, which seems to tell about the fall of the king and the failure of the Davidic covenant.

Following this, therefore, Book IV concentrates on the New Exodus out of exile and the restoration of the kingdom.[18]

---

[15] In the MT the psalmist is not identified in Psalms 66-67, and Psalm 86 is attributed to David. In the LXX only Psalm 66 (LXX 65) and Psalm 86 (LXX 85) are attributed to David.

[16] Mitchell, *The Message of the Psalter*, 71.

[17] Many scholars only recognize 42-83 as a single unit, describing it as the Elohistic Psalter, since these psalms usually refer to God as "Elohim." However, this chiastic structure shows that the collection extends through the second Korah collection. *Ibid.*, 71.

[18] Psalm 89 can be read as representing the stricken king and Book IV (90-106) as representing the ensuing exile. Mitchell, *The Message of the Psalter*, 243.

It concludes with a summary of salvation history up to the return from exile. Finally, Book V represents the restoration of the Davidic kingdom, wherein the restored tribes of Israel are united with the nations on Mount Zion praising the Lord.[19]

With this overall movement of the Psalter in mind, we shall now move into a closer examination of the flow of psalms within their respective books.

BOOK I (PSALMS 1-41)
The Law of Wisdom

Psalms 1-2 clearly form an introductory unit, which sets the tone for the whole Psalter.[20] This is highlighted by the fact that the LXX Psalter includes superscriptions for every psalm except these two.[21] Further, the link between the two psalms is evident from the blessings found at the beginning of Psalm 1 and at the end of Psalm 2. Psalm 1:1 begins, "Blessed is the man," while Psalm 2 ends, "Blessed are all who take refuge in him" (2:11). This connection has been identified in rabbinic tradition.[22]

There are other parallels as well. In Psalm 1:6 we read that "the way of the wicked will perish," while in Psalm 2:11, we find that those who do not fear the Lord will "perish in the way." Likewise, in Psalm 1:1 the blessed man "sits not in the seat of scoffers," whereas in Psalm 2:4, the Lord "sits" in heaven and laughs, scoffing at the wicked, so to speak. Finally, in Psalm

---

[19] *Ibid.*, 184-85.

[20] Patrick Miller, "The Beginning of the Psalter," *The Shape and Shaping of the Psalter*, J. Clinton McCann, ed. (Sheffield, England: Sheffield Press, 1993), 85: "[The connections between Psalms 1-2] indicate, at least on the editing level, that Psalms 1-2 were to be read together as an *entrée* into the Psalter."

[21] David Howard, "Editorial Activity in the Psalter," *The Shape and Shaping of the Psalter*, J. Clinton McCann, ed. (Sheffield, England: Sheffield Press, 1993), 58: "Most introductions and commentaries . . . note that while the Masoretic text (MT) of the Psalter carries superscriptions for only 116 psalms, the Septuagint (LXX) carries superscriptions for all but Psalms 1 and 2, lending credence [to the idea that Psalms 1-2 form an introductory unit]."

[22] See Wilson, *The Editing of the Hebrew Psalter*, 205.

1:2 the blessed man "meditates" on the law of God, while in Psalm 2:1 the same word used for "meditate"—both the Greek word in the LXX and the Hebrew word in the MT—is used for those who "plot" in vain.[23]

Psalms 1-2 are also understood by many scholars in relation to the Wisdom literature. The first psalm's contrast of the righteous and the wicked is a common theme found throughout the sapiential (wisdom) tradition. Moreover, the Edenic image of the righteous man as a tree planted by streams of water (v. 3) is much like wisdom passages such as Sirach 24, which we examined earlier. Also, the inevitable judgment of the wicked, who will be "like chaff which the wind drives away," is a theme found in the Wisdom literature, as is the idea that the blessed man walks not in the "counsel" of the wicked.

Psalm 2, like Psalm 1, depicts David as the exemplary "wise" man. As the Wisdom literature teaches, David values "fear of the Lord" and trusts that the Lord will deliver him from his earthly foes (cf. Ps. 2:10-11; Prov. 9:10).[24] As the Psalm's author, David is portrayed as the teacher of wisdom: "Now therefore, O kings, be wise; be warned, O rulers of the earth" (2:10).

The wisdom nature of Psalms 1-2 is further highlighted by its close relationship with Proverbs 1. Proverbs 1 introduces the book with many of the same themes that Psalms 1 and 2 introduce at the beginning of the Psalter. These include:

---

[23] For these three connections see Scott Harris, "Proverbs 1:8-19, 20-23 as 'Introduction,'" *Revue Biblique*, 107-2 (2000): 211-12.

[24] Sheppard, *Wisdom as a Hermeneutical Construct*, 142: "The profane nations and rulers in Ps. 2 are identified with those who walk the way of sinners and the wicked in Ps. 1. Opposite these, one finds the divine king depicted in the language of Nathan's oracle as one who, by contrastive implication, walks in the way of the righteous. Consequently, David is represented in Ps. 2 both as the author of the Psalms and also as one who qualifies under the injunction of Ps. 1 to interpret the Torah as a guide to righteousness."

- the contrast of the two ways (Ps. 1:1; 2:11; Prov. 1:15)
- the wicked as "scoffers" (Ps. 1:1; Prov. 1:22)
- description of the "righteous" (Ps. 1:5; Prov. 1:3)
- the motif of "walking" (Ps. 1:1; Prov. 1:15)
- accepting right "counsel" (Ps. 1:1; 2:2; Prov. 1:25, 30)
- the use of "torah" (Ps. 1:2; Prov. 1:8—mother's "teaching")
- "fruit" (Ps. 1:3; Prov. 1:31)
- the fear and knowledge of the Lord (Ps. 1:6; 2:10, 11; Prov. 1:7, 22, 29)
- laughing, mocking, and derision (Ps. 2:4; Prov. 1:26)[25]

From all this it seems possible to conclude that Psalms 1 and 2 introduce wisdom as the "law" to be meditated on in the five books of the Psalter. This confirms our earlier observation that wisdom is the "torah for mankind" mentioned in 2 Samuel 7:19. However, just as the Mosaic law taught not only through the words of God but also through the actions of the patriarchs, so too, the Psalter will teach Israel wisdom through the words and deeds of David. Sheppard explains:

> The entire Psalter, therefore, is made to stand theologically in association with David as a source of guidance for the way of the righteous. In this fashion, the Psalter has gained, among its other functions, the use as a source for Wisdom reflection and a model of prayers based on such a pious interpretation of the Torah.[26]

Thus, the Davidic psalms are often closely linked with some event in David's life, such as Psalm 51, which is connected with his affair with Bathsheba.

The first two psalms also introduce motifs that are especially dominant in Book I. The contrast between the wise and the foolish, the righteous and the wicked, are found in almost

---

[25] See Harris, "Proverbs 1:18-19, 20-23 as 'Introduction,'" 215-18.
[26] Sheppard, *Wisdom as a Hermeneutical Construct*, 142.

every psalm of the first Book, with David identifying himself as the former in conflict with the latter, anticipating his enemies' final destruction. In fact, nearly half of all the references to the "wicked" found in the Psalter are found in Book I.

Songs of David

Book I is predominantly a prayer of David. Nearly all of the psalms in this collection address David's struggle with his enemies and his trust in God through life-threatening ordeals.[27] Psalms 1 and 2, therefore, set the stage. There David is portrayed as the wise man who meditates on God's law (Ps. 1:1-2) and who is rescued by the Lord because he trusts in Him (Ps. 2:4-9), fearing Him rather than those who seek his life (Ps. 2:10-11).

As we saw earlier, David was connected in a special way with the *todah*. As Book I deals with the life of David—a life marked by affliction and ordeal—we discover that David frequently made *todah offerings*.[28] Book I presents David, therefore, as the wise man who relies upon fear of the Lord and *todah* sacrifice to survive ordeals.

Two psalms that are very different from the rest of those in Book I are Psalms 8 and 19. Psalm 8 describes the glory of man at the dawn of creation. It recounts how Adam was "crowned with glory and honor" and was given "dominion" over creation. Adam is portrayed as a priest-king. "Dominion" obviously relates to kingship. The crowning of "glory" and "honor" corresponds to priesthood, as Aaron is said to be crowned with "honor and glory" in Exodus 28:2.[29]

---

[27] The only psalms in Book I that do not do so are Psalms 8, 15, 19, 24, and 29.

[28] Examples of *todah* psalms are 7, 9, 26, 28, 35, and 41. Other psalms which do not contain an actual reference to "thanksgiving" and yet resemble *todah* offerings are 22, 27, 34, and 40.

[29] The two terms τιμή and δόξα occur in both Psalm 8:5 and Exodus 28:2 in the LXX.

Since David is the singer of the psalm, we can make the Adam-David connection. As we saw earlier, David fulfills the call of Adam to be a first-born priest-king. However, while Adam failed to pass his ordeal, fearing death more than God and failing to sustain himself by the tree of life (later identified as wisdom), David succeeds. Situating this Adamic psalm in the midst of the Davidic ordeal psalms may indicate David's partial fulfillment of Adam's call.

Psalm 19 is unique because of its strong emphasis on wisdom. Its role may be better understood when examined in light of Psalm 20. Together, these two psalms—situated at the center of Book I—mirror Psalms 1 and 2. Psalm 19 exalts the law of the Lord, the source of wisdom: "The law of the Lord is perfect, reviving the soul; the testimony of the Lord is sure, making wise the simple" (v. 7). Then, Psalm 20 evokes Psalm 2, speaking of the Lord's deliverance of the Davidic king from his enemies, sending support from Zion. Thus, as in Psalms 1 and 2, wisdom is connected with the victorious Davidic king.[30]

The superscriptions of the psalms are also significant because they set many of the psalms in the context of David's life. In fact, after the introductory unit of Psalms 1 and 2, Book I begins with a psalm, attributed to David, sung when he fled from Absalom. In this way, events from David's life are recounted through his prayers.

One strange psalm superscription is Psalm 30, which is attributed to David but concerns the dedication of the Temple, which David did not live to see built! We know that David first built the altar at the site of the Temple in order to avert a plague he had brought upon Israel because of his sinful census (1 Chron. 21:1-30). After the plague was averted, David decided

---

[30] See James Mays, "The Place of the Torah-Psalms in the Psalter," *Journal of Biblical Literature*, 106 (1987): 11. See also Miller, "Psalm 127—The House That Yahweh Builds," 86-87.

to build the Temple at that place (1 Chron. 22:1). This would explain why the Psalm is about deliverance, and contains no reference whatsoever to the Temple. This may also help explain why the tent of Zion was replaced. There seems to be a digression in the movement from the *todah* worship in the tent of Zion, where no curtain veiled the ark, to the Levitical cult later established in the Temple. Perhaps this was because of David's sin of the census—when David desired to be a king more than to be a priest. Hence, after the census David was afraid to go before the Lord, as he did before (1 Chron. 21:30), so he then began making plans for the Temple (1 Chron. 22:1). However, God swore His covenant oath to David in the first place because of David's desire to build a Temple. We should therefore be careful in linking the Temple to David's sin—although that connection appears to be discernable from the text.

Book I seems to wind down with the ending of David's life. Psalm 37:25 states: "I have been young, and now am old." Psalm 38 speaks of the failing of one's health in old age: "There is no soundness in my flesh . . . there is no health in my bones" (v. 3); "there is no soundness in my flesh" (v. 7); "My heart throbs, my strength fails me; and the light of my eyes—it also has gone from me. My friends and companions stand aloof from my plague" (vv. 10-11). Psalm 39 likewise seems preoccupied with the fleetingness of life and the imminence of death: "my lifetime is as nothing in thy sight . . . every man stands as a mere breath!" (v. 5); "For I am thy passing guest, a sojourner, like all my fathers. . . . Look away from me, that I may know gladness, before I depart and be no more!" (vv. 12-13).

Book I concludes with Psalm 41, which also makes references to death. It seems that David is finally on his deathbed.[31]

---

[31] The first part of the psalm speaks of the righteous man whom God delivers from his sickbed (v. 3). Verse 4, however, marks a transition, suggesting that David does not perceive that he is being delivered.

Psalm 41 indicates that David's enemies eagerly anticipate his eventual death: "When will he die, and his name perish?" (v. 5); "A deadly thing has fastened upon him; he will not rise again from where he lies" (v. 8). Finally, David asks the Lord to "raise me up," and the same word used in the LXX for "raise" is used later for the "resurrection" of Christ from the dead in the New Testament (cf. Acts 3:26).

Nevertheless, we must admit that the hypothesis that the end of Book I represents the death of David is somewhat speculative. What is clear, though, is that David is the center of Psalms 1-41. David is presented as the exemplary wise man who endures the ordeal, while faithfully trusting in the Lord and offering *todah*. Because of its fivefold division and the introductory emphasis on Torah, it is possible to see the Psalter as a kind of Davidic Torah. Like the Pentateuch, the Psalter teaches us through the words and deeds of a patriarchal figure, David. His life is recounted in the liturgical context of his psalms, particularly those for times of distress.

BOOK II (PSALMS 42-72)
The Core of Korah

Psalm 42 opens up both Book II and an interesting arrangement of psalms that extends through Book III. This structure involves the psalms of the sons of Korah (42-49), one by Asaph (50), a collection of Davidic psalms (51-72), followed by a group by Asaph (73-83), and concluding with a second collection of Korahite psalms (84-87). The fact that only one Asaph psalm appears in the first part of the arrangement, almost as a token psalm necessitated to complete the literary structure, seems to indicate deliberate editorial intent.[32]

The chronicler tells us that the descendants of Korah had important duties at the tabernacle. Moreover, David installed

---

[32] Mitchell, *The Message of the Psalter*, 90.

the Korahites as singers at the Zion tent under Heman (1 Chron. 6:31-38). Later, we are told that the Korahites were the chief guardians of the threshold of the tent, making the showbread there (1 Chron. 9:17-34). Thus, the Korahites were influential priests at the time of David.

Songs of the Community

The first Korahite collection runs from Psalms 42 to 49. The second Korahite collection appears in Book III and extends from Psalms 84 to 88, with the exception of Psalm 86, a psalm of David. It is interesting to note that a Davidic psalm stands at the center of the second collection of Korahite psalms. Further, the two Korahite collections seem to mirror each other:

Book II	Book III	Theme
42-43	84	Longing for Yahweh's dwelling place
44	85	National lament
46, 48	87	"Song of Zion"

Though Psalms 45, 47, and 86 are not related, it is hard to imagine that this arrangement is accidental.[33]

In contrast to Book I, which was dominated by individual prayers, the Korahite collection (as well as most of the psalms in Books II-III) is composed of songs of the community. The Korahite psalms also contain their own vocabulary. For example, God's people are consistently referred to as "Jacob," not "Israel" (Ps. 44:4; 46:7, 11; 84:8; 85:1; 87:2). The only appearance in the Psalter of the phrase "the living God" is in the Korahite collections (42:2; 84:2). The Korahite psalms are also the only place where the term "oppression" occurs in the Psalter (42:9; 43:2; 44:24). The phrase "city of God" is unique

---

[33] Michael D. Goulder, *The Psalms of the Sons of Korah* (Sheffield, England: Sheffield Press, 1982), 12.

to the Korahite collection as well (46:4; 48:1; 87:3—"city of our God" only occurs in 48:8).[34]

Book II opens up with a pair of introductory psalms, much like Book I. These psalms are generally recognized by scholars as being related.[35] Psalm 43 picks up the refrain used in Psalm 42: "Why are you cast down, O my soul, and why are you disquieted within me? Hope in God; for I shall again praise him, my help and my God" (Ps. 42:5-6, 11; Ps. 43:5). Both psalms ask: "Why go I mourning because of the oppression of the enemy?" (Ps. 42:9; Ps. 43:2). In addition, both psalms speak of being forgotten or cast off by God (cf. Ps. 42:9; 43:2), and each speaks of going to the sanctuary of the Lord (cf. Ps. 42:4; 43:3).

Psalm 42 also seems to be closely connected with the experience of the northern tribes. For example, 42:7 mentions Mount Herman, located in the northern kingdom. Because of this, some scholars conclude that this psalm is northern in origin.[36]

Psalms 42 and 43 set the stage for Psalm 44. While Psalms 42 and 43 speak of an individual being abandoned by God, Psalm 44 translates that into the collective experience of Israel's going into exile. In fact, scholars discern exile imagery in Psalms 42 and 43.[37] We can also draw several literary links between Psalms 42 and 44:

---

[34] *Ibid.*, 3.

[35] For example, see Howard, "Editorial Activity in the Psalter," 67; Wilson, *The Editing of the Hebrew Psalter*, 173-76; Mitchell, *The Message of the Psalter*, 29; Jerome F.D. Creach, *Yahweh As Refuge and the Editing of the Hebrew Psalter*, 86; Gary A. Rendsburg, *Linguistic Evidence for the Northern Origin of Selected Psalms* (Atlanta: Scholars Press, 1990), 59; and Mays, "The Place of the Torah—Psalms in the Psalter," 173-76.

[36] Rendsburg, *Linguistic Evidence for the Northern Origin of Selected Psalms*, 59.

[37] Mitchell, *The Message of the Psalter*, 250: "Psalms 42 and 43 represent Israel in exile, separated from the temple (42:3-5 [2-4]), taunted by the heathen, crying to God for redemption, and anticipating its coming (42:10-11 [1-3]), celebrates God's saving power (5-9 [4-8]), laments Israel's sorrows that God has brought upon them (10-23 [9-22]), and culminates with a plea that God redeem them (vv. 24-27 [23-26]) presumably just as he formerly did at the exodus, by leading them out of heathen oppression to the promised land."

- "To the choirmaster. A Maskil of the Sons of Korah"
  (Ps. 42; 44)
- People, individual are taunted by their enemies
  (Ps. 42:10; 43:2; 44:24)
- People, individual are "oppressed" (Ps. 42:9; 43:2; 44:24)
- People, individual are both "cast off" (Ps. 43:2; 44:9)
- People, individual are "forgotten" (Ps. 42:9; 44:20)
- People, individual cannot see the face of God
  (Ps. 42:3; 44:24)
- Soul being brought low or "cast down"
  (Ps. 42:5-6, 11; 43:5; 44:25)

Book II, therefore, marks a transition. If the psalms in Book I are primarily ordeal psalms of an individual, Books II and III are principally couched in the collective experience of the exile. However, while this is generally an accurate description, this claim must be held with a loose grip. Psalm 14 asks God to restore "the fortunes of his people" (v. 7), and Psalm 25 similarly states, "Redeem Israel, O God, out of all his troubles" (v. 22). Although the exile may be read into these psalms, it is extremely interesting that exile is *never* clearly expressed in Book I.

Psalm 45 is clearly a psalm about the Davidic king and seems to be a wedding psalm.[38] Interestingly, some scholars, like Gary Rendsburg, see the psalm as northern in origin, which would provide another link to the two previous psalms.[39] Mitchell sees the placement of this psalm after the plea from exile as an indication of God's plan to restore Israel under the Davidic

---

[38] Mays, "The Place of the Torah-Psalms in the Psalter," 45; Mitchell, *The Message of the Psalter*, 268.

[39] Rendsburg points, for instance, to the interesting use of the Hebrew word *hekal*: "Twice in this psalm the word *hekal* is used to mean 'palace,' as opposed to its usual meaning 'temple,' in the expressions *hekele sen*, 'palaces of ivory,' in v. 9 and *hekal melek*, 'palace of the king,' in v. 16. An examination of other biblical usages of *hekal* = 'palace' reveals this to be a northern idiom," *Linguistic Evidence for the Northern Origin of Selected Psalms*, 47.

king: "Psalms 42-43 represent Israel in exile. . . . Psalm 45 therefore becomes the answer to this prayer, revealing the redeemer,
the bridegroom-king, who will turn Israel's sorrow to joy."[40]

Furthermore, Mitchell shows how the content of Psalms 44
and 45 is much like the scheme of Zechariah 9-11. There
Israel is described as gathered from exile where they have been
"scattered" (Zech. 10:9; 13:7; Ps. 44:8) by a Davidic king
(Zech. 2:7-10; 12:7-14; Psalm 45), who comes "riding" in
(Zech. 9:9; Ps. 45:4) as a bridegroom to a daughter/bride
(Zech. 9:9; Ps. 45:10).[41]

Arguably, the most intriguing part of Psalm 45 is its declaration, "Your divine throne endures for ever and ever" (v. 6).
While some scholars assert that this statement is directed to
Yahweh, this does not seem to be the case. Indeed, *all* ancient
versions of this passage outside of the Masoretic Text understand this as a statement directed to the Davidic king,
including the Septuagint, the Targums, the New Testament
Book of Hebrews, Aquila, Summachus, the Peshitta, and the
Vulgate.[42] Hence, the kingship of David is inextricably linked
to the kingship of God. This connection is made in 1
Chronicles 28:5: "[The Lord] has chosen Solomon my son to
sit upon the throne of the kingdom of the LORD." Likewise,
the Davidic kingdom is clearly understood as the kingdom of
God: "[N]ow you think to withstand the kingdom of the
LORD in the hand of the sons of David" (2 Chron. 13:8).

The close connection of the throne of David and the kingship of God is especially seen in the description of Zion as
both the city of David and the city of God. Hence, Zion is
referred to as the "city of God" in Psalm 46:4. Psalm 47, then,
is a psalm of God's kingship. This is followed by a song of

---

[40] Mitchell, *The Message of the Psalter*, 250.
[41] *Ibid.*, 249-50.
[42] *Ibid.*, 246.

Zion in Psalm 48. Thus, a certain kingship/Zion interlocking pattern is formed:[43]

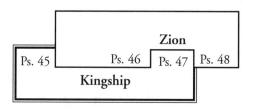

Mount Zion manifests the union of the kingship of God with the Davidic dynasty. There is no tension between the two. God reigns through the Davidic king.

Further, since it was through Solomon that the nations were brought into covenant with Yahweh, particularly through his diplomatic marriages, the psalms following the Davidic wedding of Psalm 45 emphasize Yahweh's reign over the nations. Moreover, it would seem that the restoration of Israel through the Davidic king is closely connected here with the international element of the New Exodus. Thus, Psalms 46-49 clearly demonstrate God's kingship over all nations. This is in stark contrast to Psalms 42-44, which hold out no hope for an international recognition of Yahweh as the one true God and King.

The first Korahite collection (Psalms 42-49) ends as it began, with an individual's psalm of distress. Psalm 49 is also noteworthy because of its emphasis on wisdom. Those who are wise will be saved "from the power of Sheol" (v. 15), whereas the wicked will have their home in their graves forever (v. 11). Hence, wisdom can deliver one from death. The Davidic ordeal thus resonates with the Adamic trial. Perhaps this hope of overcoming the grave is connected with the hope of being delivered from exile, because resurrection was so

---

[43] See Creach, *Yahweh As Refuge and the Editing of the Hebrew Psalter*, 87.

closely associated with the restoration. In other words, Israel faces a life-threatening ordeal corporately, as Adam and David faced individually. Wisdom is the way they will be able to endure it redemptively.

Gather Us In

Psalm 50 is the only Asaph psalm in Book II. Asaph was the head priest in the Davidic Zion tent, in which the *todah* sacrifice was offered instead of the sin offering. Asaph led the singing of the songs of thanksgiving (cf. 1 Chron. 16). Further, the sons of Asaph seem to have been recognized as having a prophetic charism (cf. 1 Chron. 25:1; 2 Chron. 20:14-17). Mitchell explains:

> [T]he role of the non-priestly Asaphites was probably not that of sounding the hazozerot. Instead, as levitical prophet-musicians, their role may have been to chant petitions and prophetic oracles appropriate to the occasion as Jahaziel in Jehosophat's time, or to sound the *shofar*.[44]

The sons of Asaph, therefore, sang songs of *todah* and prophesied. Like Jahaziel's prophecy, which foretold of an invasion by a foreign power, many of the Asaphite psalms deal with the threat of an attack by the nations.[45]

"Asaph" literally means "to gather." Predictably, this theme arises in the Asaphite Psalm 50. Indeed, some early Christian commentators translate the Asaphite psalms as "For the ingathering."[46] It would seem that "Asaph" is closely related to the name of Joseph etymologically, which combines the

---

[44] Mitchell, *The Message of the Psalter*, 96.

[45] This is especially clear in the LXX superscriptions of Psalms 76 and 80, which identify themselves as psalms concerning the Assyrians. Other instances of foreign invasion in the Asaph psalms are 74:3; 79:1-3; and 83:5-6.

[46] Mitchell, *The Message of the Psalter*, 99.

Hebrew roots "God has ingathered" and "Yahweh will add."[47] Joseph, son of Jacob, is portrayed as one who gathered together the harvest of the earth in Genesis 41:48, as well as the heads of the twelve tribes in Genesis 42:17. Also, one of Asaph's sons was named Joseph (cf. 1 Chron. 25:2). With the exception of Psalm 105, which is a summary of Israel's history, all the references to Joseph in the Psalter are in the Asaph psalms. The Patriarch Jacob is also frequently mentioned in the Asaph collection. This could relate to the fact that Jacob gathered the twelve tribal heads around his bedside before his death, issuing prophecy concerning each of them (cf. Gen. 49:1 *et seq.*).

Earlier we saw evidence that some of the Korahite psalms may have roots in northern Israel. There is also evidence to support northern elements in the Asaph psalms. For example, northern Israel's victories over foreign enemies seem to be hinted at in Psalm 83.[48]

It is possible to see Psalm 50 in connection with the last Asaph psalm, Psalm 83. Psalm 50 warns Israel that God will bring judgment against them, which is accomplished by the attack of the ten-nation confederation in Psalm 83. Psalm 50:3-5 depicts God as coming in judgment in a devouring fire. Psalm 83:14 portrays God pursuing the enemies of Israel "[a]s fire consumes the forest." Likewise, Psalm 50:15 exhorts Israel to call upon the Lord in the day of trouble, which aptly describes the setting of Psalm 83.

Since Asaph was the chief singer of the *todah*, it should not be surprising that Psalm 50 condemns Israel's burnt offerings, telling them instead, "Offer to God a sacrifice of thanksgiving" (v. 14). Psalm 50 explains that God does not primarily desire animal sacrifice. Instead, He wants to teach Israel to call upon

---

[47] *Ibid.*, 101.
[48] *Ibid.*, 80; Rendsburg, *Linguistic Evidence for the Northern Origin of Selected Psalms*, 73.

Him in times of trouble (v. 15). The *todah* is therefore the appropriate response to the ordeal. Further, Psalm 50 portrays God as the One who is bringing judgment on Israel. Thus, God allows "the day of trouble" to befall Israel so that the people may learn to offer true sacrifice: "He who brings thanksgiving as his sacrifice honors me" (v. 23).

Sing Along with David

Following Psalm 50, the second Davidic collection begins (51-72). The superscription for Psalm 51 presents the psalm as David's penitential prayer following his affair with Bathsheba. This psalm is connected with Psalm 50 in its description of the inadequacy of the sin offering. Psalm 50 condemns the burnt offerings of sinful Israel: "[Y]our burnt offerings are continually before me. I will accept no bull from your house, nor he-goat from your folds" (vv. 8-9). Similarly, David recognizes the insufficiency of his holocausts: "For thou hast no delight in sacrifice; were I to give a burnt offering, thou wouldst not be pleased" (51:16). The parallels in the description seem too striking to be accidental. In fact, Psalm 50 condemns Israel for keeping "company with adulterers" (v. 18), which also links it to Psalm 51, sung after David's adulterous affair with Bathsheba.

Yet, Psalm 51 inserts a curious line: "rebuild the walls of Jerusalem" (v. 18). This does not make sense coming forth from David. Surely, no one would expect David to be praying for restoration, since that would be anachronistic. Instead, David is presented as an example for Israel. His life of suffering and repentance gives Israel in exile a model to follow. Hence, Books II-III have a deliberate structure that underscores the centrality of the Davidic collection, presenting David as an example for corporate Israel, much like Psalm 2 presents David as the ideal wise man of Psalm 1. In this the Davidic aspect of the restoration is clearly highlighted.

Psalm 52 flows from the previous psalm. In Psalm 51, David tells the Lord that once he is forgiven he will "teach transgressors thy ways" (v. 13). Psalm 52 then begins with an address to the wicked: "Why do you boast, O mighty man, of mischief done against the godly" (v. 1). Almost as if they have rejected the words of David, the psalms that immediately follow depict the wicked, not converting, but rather seeking the life of David.

Like Psalm 50, these psalms show that the wicked are not only the Gentiles, but also the Israelites. Psalms 52 and 54 describe David's flight from Saul. Psalm 53 explains, "They have all fallen away" (v. 3). In other words, David is saying, "Israelites and Gentiles are against me—no one nation has 'cornered the market' when it comes to sin." Psalm 55 explains:

> It is not an enemy who taunts me—then I could bear it; it is not an adversary who deals insolently with me—then I could hide from him. But it is you, my equal, my companion, my familiar friend, We used to hold sweet converse together; within God's house we walked in fellowship. . . . My companion stretched out his hand against his friends, he violated his covenant (vv. 12-14, 20).

Hence, David's struggles with Israelites, particularly with Saul, are presented side by side with psalms about the Philistines throughout the second Davidic collection.

In fact, Saul is a recurring figure in the superscriptions. A summary of Psalms 52-57 would appear something like this:

52   David flees from Saul.
53   No one nation is righteous, not even Israel.
54   David flees from Saul.
55   David is threatened by his "companion."
56   David is pursued by the Philistines.
57   David flees from Saul.

This arrangement vividly illustrates that a major theme in David's life was not only his struggle with the Gentiles, but also with his fellow Israelites, who had rebelled against the Lord and His anointed one.

Psalm 58 goes on to ask the Lord for deliverance, petitioning Him to crush the wicked. Next, Psalm 59 explains the result of such vindication. David's concern is not merely the sparing of his own life, but also the slaying of the wicked, so "that men may know that God rules over Jacob to the ends of the earth" (v. 13). Hence, in the Lord's deliverance of David, the nations will come to acknowledge the Lord as God. Psalms 61-64 are lament psalms, continuing the prayer for deliverance.

The theme of lament is dropped in Psalms 65-68, as Israel is joined by the nations in the worship of the Lord on Zion. Of course, the glorious gathering of "all flesh" in praise on Zion never happened in David's lifetime. Thus, these psalms must be seen as reflecting the hope of Israel, which is presented in the Psalter as the hope of David.

The theme of the *todah* may also be found in these psalms. The unification of Israel in praise with the nations is implied by the result of David/Israel's *todah* ordeal experience. Psalm 65:1-2 explains:

> Praise is due to thee, O God, in Zion; and to thee shall vows be performed, O thou who hearest prayer! To thee all flesh shall come on account of sins.

This seems to evoke *todah* imagery. Praise is due and the vow to sacrifice will be fulfilled because God has heard the prayer for deliverance. Moreover, because of God's vindication and the subsequent offering of sacrifice, "all flesh" shall come in repentance. One cannot help but think of the eschatological feast with all the nations on Zion as described in Isaiah 25:6-8.

Todah imagery is also found in Psalm 66: "I will come into thy house with burnt offerings; I will pay thee my vows" (v. 13). This psalm explains that Israel's affliction was meant as a test: "For thou, O God, hast tested us; thou hast tried us as silver is tried" (v. 10). As a result of God's fatherly discipline, Israel is restored to its vocation to call the nations back to the Lord: "Make a joyful noise to God, all the earth . . . All the earth worships thee . . . Bless our God, O peoples" (vv. 1, 4, 8). Psalm 67 continues this "catholic" worship, as it emphasizes the worship of "all the peoples" (vv. 3, 5).

Psalm 67 explains that God's deliverance of Israel will allow the way of the Lord to "be known upon earth, the saving power among all the nations" (v. 2). Indeed, every line of the psalm, with the exception of the first verse, refers to this universal worship of God, repeating the refrain "let all the peoples praise thee" (vv. 3, 5). The psalm concludes, "let all the ends of the earth fear him" (v. 7).

Psalm 68 is the climactic song of universal worship of God on Zion. It begins by recounting the Lord's deliverance of His people: "Let God arise, let his enemies be scattered" (v. 1). There's an ironic twist here since Israel itself ended up rejecting God and being "scattered" to the nations. The psalm goes on to reflect the movement from Sinai to Zion (vv. 15-18), where Israel and all the nations come to worship God.[49] This psalm also depicts the sacrifice of the Temple as a ritual enactment of God's judgment on the gods who had formerly held Israel captive, as we saw earlier. This sacrifice itself expresses the hope of restoration.

After Psalm 68, the lament psalms resume from 69 to 71. Psalm 69 is clearly a *todah* psalm. Like Psalm 51, it is ascribed

---

[49] All Israel is depicted in the mention of the tribes of Benjamin and Judah, the two southern tribes, and Zebulun and Naphtali, two of the northernmost tribes.

to David, but contains an exilic statement: "For God will save
Zion and rebuild the cities of Judah" (v. 35). Hence, David's
suffering is clearly linked to Israel's. Psalm 70, which follows,
also depicts an ordeal of David.

Psalm 71, like the end of Book I, seems to portray an older
David who looks back on his life of suffering. Verse 9 reads:
"Do not cast me off in the time of old age, forsake me not
when my strength is spent." Likewise, Psalm 71:17-18 provides: "O God, from my youth thou hast taught me, and I
still proclaim thy wondrous deeds. So even to old age and
gray hairs, O God, do not forsake me." The psalm even seems
to hint at resurrection: "Thou who hast made me see many
sore troubles wilt revive me again; from the depths of the earth
thou wilt bring me up again" (Ps. 71:20). This is similar to
Psalm 41:10, which also seemed to hint at resurrection. As in
Book I, David is chased and pursued even out into the
desert—in a sense, exiled himself—giving an example to
Israel in its suffering.

Book II concludes with a psalm for Solomon.[50] David
prays that his aspirations to unite the nations and the
promise made to Abraham in Genesis 22 will be realized in
Solomon's reign.[51] Indeed, the Solomonic era was a kind of
partial fulfillment of God's plan to bring the nations back to
Him. Through his marriages Solomon brought the nations
into covenant relationship with Yahweh. The Temple he
constructed had a special court for the nations to worship.
Thus, the psalm's postscript reads: "The prayers of David,
the son of Jesse, are ended" (Ps. 72:20). This is not to be
understood as marking the end of an older form of the

[50] See the discussion of the superscription on p. 84, *supra*.
[51] In Genesis 22:18, God swears by Himself that "by your descendants shall all the
nations of the earth bless themselves, because you have obeyed my voice," which is
echoed in Psalm 72:17: "May men bless themselves by him."

Psalter, but rather as the fulfillment of David's hopes and dreams—the accomplishment of David's prayer.[52]

However, Solomon's heart turned away from the Lord, and thus Solomon proved not to be the object of the ultimate hope of Israel. Rather, the Solomonic golden age serves as an icon that points to the restoration of the Davidic kingdom. Therefore, the psalm should be interpreted as the hope of exiled Israel. The Peshitta thus renders the heading of Psalm 72: "A Psalm of David, when he had made Solomon king, and a prophecy concerning the advent of the Messiah and the calling of the Gentiles."[53]

BOOK III (PSALMS 73-89)
Facing Reality

To underscore the exilic condition of Israel and to clarify that the awaited messianic kingdom has not yet come to pass, Book III begins with a psalm of lament. Indeed, in stark contrast to the conclusion of Book II, Book III contains a high concentration of exilic psalms: 74, 77, 79, 80, 83, 85, and 89.[54] Psalm 73 sets up this dichotomy.

Psalm 73 marks the beginning of an Asaph collection. It has strong thematic and literary links with Psalm 72. While Psalm 72 envisioned a universal kingdom of peace, justice, and freedom from oppression, Psalm 73 "brings the reader back to the hard reality of the present."[55]

Several terms are shared by both psalms, indicating that the latter is a response to the former. Psalms scholar Robert

---

[52] This is common in Rabbinic interpretation. Mitchell cites Rashi who stated: "And are not the remaining prayers also prayers of David ben Jesse? *Kalu*, however, is to be read *kol 'ellu*. And hence the verse means that all of these [*kol 'ellu*] were the prayers David uttered concerning his son Solomon and concerning King Messiah." Mitchell, *The Message of the Psalter*, 68.

[53] *Ibid.*, 21.

[54] McCann, "Books I-III and the Editorial Purpose of the Psalter," 98.

[55] Cole, *The Shape and Message of Book III*, 15.

Cole shows that many of the same Hebrew words used in 72 recur in 73.[56] The righteousness, justice, and peace which are idealized in Psalm 72 (vv. 1-2, 7) have not been realized. Instead, the wicked dwell in peace (Ps. 73:3-4, 12). Though Psalm 72:3 promised the prosperity of Israel, in Psalm 73:3 the wicked dwell in prosperity. While Psalm 72 promised to give deliverance from oppression (v. 4), describing God's enemies as "licking the dust" (v. 9), Psalm 73 describes the violence of the wicked (v. 6), who continue to threaten the people of God (v. 8). Psalm 72 says that the peoples will offer prayers for Solomon "all the day," but in Psalm 73, the righteous are stricken "all the day long" (v. 14). Instead of blessing God, they say, "How can God know? Is there knowledge in the Most High?" (v. 11).

Psalm 73 may also be linked to Psalms 1-2.[57] Psalm 73 looks at the wicked and shows that they will eventually be destroyed, as Psalms 1-2 warn (vv. 18-20, 27).[58] Moreover, just as Psalm 3 is a lament psalm, which follows the triumphal image of the Davidic king in Psalm 2, Psalm 73 is a lament psalm that follows a similar idealistic portrayal in Psalm 72.

Psalm 73 is then linked with Psalm 74. The individual in Psalm 73 was comforted when he "went into the sanctuary of God; then I perceived their end" (v. 17). Yet, even this consolation is taken away in Psalm 74: "the enemy has destroyed everything in the sanctuary! . . . They set thy sanctuary on fire; to the ground they desecrated the dwelling place of thy name" (vv. 3, 7). In Psalm 73:9 the wicked "set their mouths against the heavens." Similarly, in Psalm 74:18 we read that, "the enemy scoffs, and an impious people reviles thy name."

---

[56] *Ibid.*
[57] Walter Brueggemann and Patrick Miller, "Psalm 73 as a Canonical Marker," *Journal for the Study of the Old Testament*, 72 (1996): 48-52.
[58] Cole, *The Shape and Message of Book III*, 26.

Psalm 74 also continues the concern of Psalm 73 for the "poor" and the "needy" (vv. 19, 21).[59]

It would also seem that Psalm 74 is an indictment of the wickedness of Israel. In Psalm 73:19, the destruction of the wicked is foretold. In Psalm 74, Israel is the wicked nation who experiences this destruction. Nonetheless, the psalmist appeals to the covenant of Yahweh as the basis for Israel's hope of deliverance and restoration: "Have regard for thy covenant" (v. 20).

Psalm 75 seems to be a response to the previous two psalms. It begins by offering thanksgiving. This suggests a *todah*, which is made in the midst of affliction. Psalm 74 asked, "O God, why dost thou cast us off for ever?" Psalm 75:2 gives God's answer: "At the set time which I will appoint I will judge with equity." In other words, He will not forget them *forever*.[60] Likewise, a connection can be found between Psalm 74:11, which asks, "Why dost thou hold back thy hand?" and Psalm 75:8, which speaks of the cup that will be poured out on the wicked, which is held "in the hand of the LORD." It would also seem that the references in Psalm 75:4-5 to the wicked, who are "boastful" and speak with an "insolent neck," echo Psalm 73, which spoke of the necklace of pride of the wicked (v. 5), who also spoke arrogantly against the Lord (vv. 8-9).

Psalm 76 is a Zion psalm, recounting the hoped for restoration of Israel on the holy mountain of God. It seems that the *todah* is implied by verse 11: "Make your vows to the Lord your God and perform them." If this is a reference to the *todah*, we see yet another instance in which the *todah* is linked to the restoration of Israel on Zion. Further, the psalm's statement, "let all around him bring gifts to him who

[59] *Ibid.*, 27-30.
[60] *Ibid.*, 38.

is to be feared" (v. 11), seems to be an allusion to the inter-national character of the restoration.[61]

As Psalm 73 is a lament following the hopeful Psalm 72, a song of lament follows Psalm 76. Here the complaints of the unfulfilled promise of the kingdom are explicitly stated:

> Will the Lord spurn for ever, and never again be favorable? Has his steadfast love for ever ceased? Are his promises at an end for all time? Has God forgotten to be gracious? Has he in anger shut up his compassion? And I say, "It is my grief that the right hand of the Most High has changed" (Ps. 77:7-10).

The psalmist then recalls the events of the Exodus (vv.11-20). Implied in this recollection of God's miraculous deliverance of Israel from Egypt is the hope for a New Exodus, in which God will miraculously rescue Israel from the nations.

Holy Nostalgia

Psalm 78 provides one of the most insightful descriptions of God's dealings with Israel in all of Scripture. It begins by recounting how the Lord brought Israel up out of Egypt through wondrous signs (v. 4). It goes on to tell how, after the Israelites sinned, He gave the first generation the Law to teach their children, so that they would not forget Him (vv. 5-8). Yet, the second generation was no better than the first, and the more God worked miracles for them, the more they sinned against Him (vv. 9-17). Israel spoke against the Lord, complaining that God had brought them out into the wilderness only to starve them to death (vv. 18-20). So God, to prove

---

[61] *Ibid.*, 52: "The phrase 'all who surround him' in 76:12 certainly includes those in Judah and Zion of vv. 2-3, but also others who are commanded to bring homage. Kings are mentioned directly in the following 76:13, presumably included among those bearing gifts. Such a scenario again recalls Psalm 72 directly."

His trustworthiness, gave them everything they asked for (vv. 21-29), but they still rebelled against Him (v. 32). So God began to slay them, and in so doing they finally sought after Him and repented earnestly (vv. 33-34).

But this repentance was short lived. Psalm 78 goes on to explain how the people continued to rebel and provoke God once they entered into the Promised Land, despite all the wondrous things He did for them (vv. 35-55). So the Lord allowed them to be taken into captivity and gave them up to their enemies, even allowing the ark of the covenant to be taken away from them (vv. 56-64). Nevertheless, after a little while, the Lord redeemed His people and saved them through His servant David, elevating the tribe of Judah and making His dwelling on Zion (vv. 67-72).

The psalm's description of Israel's captivity and deliverance certainly has implications for the exiled Israelites' hope for the restoration of the Davidic kingdom. Psalm 78 also draws a sharp contrast between the house of Ephraim and the house of Judah. Ephraim was the son of Joseph who received the blessing of the first-born from his grandfather Jacob (Israel) in Genesis 48:14-20. As such, it would seem that Israel's monarchy should belong to the house of Ephraim.[62]

However, Deuteronomy 21 explains that if a man has two wives and has a son through each of them, he may not give the first-born blessing to the son of the wife he loves most if he was not born first (cf. Deut. 21:15-17). Ephraim was the son of Joseph, who was born of Jacob's favorite wife (Rachel). Judah was born to the wife Jacob disliked (Leah), but was

---

[62] The election of Judah is even more surprising since Judah was Jacob's fourth born. Yet Reuben defiled himself in Genesis 35 by lying with his father's concubine. Thus, he is condemned by Jacob before he died. Simeon and Levi likewise violently avenged the rape of their sister Dinah in Genesis 34, causing Jacob to curse them as well. Hence, Judah was the first son to receive a blessing from his father, receiving the promise of the "scepter."

older than Joseph. So even though he was born of the disliked wife, he could not be bypassed because he was older.
Nonetheless, though Judah was given the monarchy (since
David was from the tribe of Judah), the double blessing
given to Ephraim did play out in the fact that Ephraim
always existed as Israel's strongest and wealthiest tribe.
Indeed, when the north broke from the south, an Ephraimite
was made king.

Psalm 78 also answers the complaint of Psalm 77:7-10 that
God has seemed to abandon His people. The psalmist shows
that God has historically drawn away from the Israelites to
punish them for their sin. Thus, the punishment Israel is
experiencing in the present is not a sign of God's betrayal of
Israel, but His fatherly discipline. Indeed, it is Israel, not God,
who continually rejects the covenant.[63]

The psalmist further explains that the people only turned to
repentance after the Lord began to slay them (Ps. 78:33-34). In
this we see that David's desire to conquer his enemies and the
Lord's punishment of even His own people have a redemptive
purpose. God is a loving Father. He does not enjoy killing His
people. Even so, He knows that sometimes people are so
hardened in sin that it takes something drastic or threatening
to lead them to repentence. In the grand scheme, then, God's
wrath is actually mercy. He chastises and sends suffering to
wake up His people from their sin. This is similar to Psalm 59,
where David prays that the wicked will be destroyed so that
"men may know that God rules" (v. 13).

Psalm 79 is a kind of corporate lament and *todah*. It again
contrasts the promises of the Davidic kingdom and Zion with
the reality of Israel in exile. If Israel is God's "inheritance"
(78:71), why have the nations been allowed to overcome

---

[63] Cole, *The Shape and Message of Book III*, 76: "Psalm 78 has responded to 77's
lament concerning continual divine anger by pointing out that Israel's rebellion was
continual as well."

them (79:1)?[64] If God has loved Zion so much and has made it His sanctuary (78:69), why has God allowed His Temple to be defiled and destroyed (Ps. 79:1)? Like many of the Davidic psalms, it ends with a promise to offer *todah* once the restoration has occurred (v. 13).

Psalms 78 and 79 have discernible parallels. Psalm 78 begins by addressing "the following generation" (v. 4), while Psalm 79:13 speaks of thanks being given "from generation to generation." Similarly, the end of Psalm 79 repeats many of the concluding elements of Psalm 78: Israel is God's people (78:71; 79:13), who are portrayed as God's sheep (78:70; 79:13).

Psalm 80 is a lament that continues the cries of Psalm 79. The major refrain of this psalm, "Restore us, O God," is a clear reference to the hope of the New Exodus. Exodus imagery is used in this psalm as it was in Psalms 77 and 78. Moreover, the shepherd imagery used in Psalms 77:20, 78:70-71, and 79:13 is present at the outset of the psalm, showing continuity with the preceding psalms. Further, Psalm 79 asks "How long" (v. 5) and "why" (v. 10), which is repeated in Psalm 80:4, 12.

Psalm 80 also hints at the connection of God's kingship over Israel with the reign of the Davidic king. While Psalm 78:70-71 referred to David as the shepherd of Israel, Psalm 80:1 describes God in those terms. Yet, the psalm also makes reference to the "man of thy right hand" (80:17), presumably the Davidic king, through whom restoration will be accomplished (cf. Ps. 110:1).

One other interesting aspect of Psalm 80 is the reference to "the son of man whom thou hast made strong for thyself!" (v. 17). This "son" seems to be a reference back to the Davidic king, who is described in terms of sonship in Psalms 2:7, 72:1,

---

[64] In fact, while Psalm 78 ends with Israel as God's inheritance, Psalm 79 begins by reminding the Lord that He has allowed the nations to defile His inheritance.

89:27, and 132:11.[65] So then, this "son of man" is presented as
the one who will accomplish the restoration of the kingdom.
This is very much like the "son of man" in Daniel 7:13-14:

> there came one like a son of man, and he came to the Ancient
> of Days and was presented before him. And to him was given
> dominion and glory and kingdom . . . his dominion is an
> everlasting dominion . . . and his kingdom one that shall not
> be destroyed.

Thus, in both Psalm 80:17 and Daniel 7:13-14, "the son of
man" is portrayed as the one who will ultimately restore the
kingdom to Israel.[66]

Psalm 81 serves as an answer to the lament of the previous
psalms. It employs Exodus imagery, warning the people of
Israel not to turn their hearts away from Him as their fathers
had (vv. 5-10). Further, God explains to Israel that it is
because of their sins that enemies besiege them, not because
God has forgotten them (vv. 11-14). The LXX superscription
for this psalm, as well as that for Psalms 8 and 83, reads "for
the wine presses." Hence, God's judgment is likened to the
wrath of the Lord in Isaiah 63:3-4:

> I have trodden the wine press alone, and from the peoples no
> one was with me; . . . For the day of vengeance was in my
> heart, and my year of redemption has come.[67]

While Psalm 80:17 asks God to place His "hand" on the
Davidic king to restore Israel, in Psalm 81:14 God will turn
His "hand" against their enemies. The psalmist asks God to

---

[65] Cole, *The Shape and Message of Book III*, 89.
[66] In fact, the Targum of Psalm 80 interprets this "son of man" as the coming
messianic king. See Schaper, *Eschatology in the Greek Psalter*, 98.
[67] All three psalms that bear this superscription follow a psalm about judgment.
See Mitchell, *The Message of the Psalter*, 189.

"turn again" to help Israel in 80:14, while here he speaks of God's "turning" against Israel's oppressors. Instead of "feeding" His people with tears (Ps. 80:5), God will "feed" His people with finest wheat (Ps. 81:16). The reference in 81:9 to "strange gods" may also serve as a link to Psalm 82, where God judges the "gods" who have oppressed Israel, thus answering the cries of affliction.

Hoping Against Hope

Skipping over Psalm 83, which we examined at in our treatment of Asaph Psalm 50, we will now turn our attention to the second Korahite collection. This collection follows the pattern of the first group of Korah psalms very closely.[68] The hope for restoration of the kingdom plays a dominant role in these psalms. Mitchell summarizes these psalms:

> [T]he end of Book III seems full of hopes for a new beginning. Psalm 82:8 calls on God to judge the earth. Psalm 83 shows the judgment imminent and implies the coming victory (10-19 [9-18]). Psalm 84 speaks of the blessedness of Zion, and requests God's favor on his *mashiah*. Psalm 85 promises the restoration of the land. Psalm 87 celebrates Zion. And then follows the horror of Psalms 88 and 89.[69]

Psalm 84 is a Zion song. Its setting within the context of exile psalms seems to indicate its role as a song of hope for the restoration of the kingdom. Indeed, the Targum to 84:9 reads: "See, O God, the righteousness of our fathers, and look upon the face of your Messiah."[70]

---

[68] See previous treatment of Korah psalms 42-49 on pp. 93-98, *supra*.
[69] Mitchell, *The Message of the Psalter*, 80.
[70] Mitchell also suggests that the original setting for Psalms 83 and 84 is the Assyrian invasion of the north and the south. First, the forming of the alliance through which Assyria destroyed the northern kingdom is announced in Psalm 83 (v. 8, "Assyria also has joined them . . ."). Then, the southern kingdom's praise of God for sparing Zion from Sennacherib's army is reflected in Psalm 84. This, however, seems to involve more eisegesis than exegesis. *Ibid.*, 257.

Psalm 85 is another psalm asking God to restore Israel, begging Him to "revive us again" (v. 6). Here, as we have seen elsewhere, a kind of resurrection motif functions for the hope of the restoration. This request to bring Israel back to life may be linked to the opening of Psalm 84, which describes the Lord as "the living God" (v. 2). In fact, the speaker of Psalm 84 seems to refer to a kind of lifelessness for himself: "My soul longs, yea faints for the courts of the LORD" (v. 2).[71]

Psalm 86, a prayer of David, shares many connections with Psalm 72:

Psalm 72	Psalm 86
"May he defend the cause of the poor . . . [and] give deliverance to the needy" (v. 4)	"for I am poor and needy" (v. 1)
"May his foes bow down before him" (v. 9)	"bow down before thee, O Lord" (v. 9)
"For he delivers the needy when he calls" (v. 12)	"In the day of trouble I call on thee, for thou dost answer me" (v. 7)

Thus, this Psalm 86 is a lament psalm based on the non-fulfillment of the prayer for Solomon in Psalm 72. It places the hope of future fulfillment in the coming Davidic king who will bring about the restoration of Israel with the nations. "Not by coincidence [Psalm 86] contains the most parallels with Psalm 72 and its description of the eschatological kingdom."[72]

---

[71] Cole, *The Shape and Message of Book III*, 126: "Part of the plea in Psalm 85 is for God to again bring life to the nations (v. 7), a request that only the living God (84.3) is capable of answering. Lifelessness has been expressed already by the individual in 84.3, whose soul is spent, but found strength in Yahweh (84.6), and trusted in him (84.13). Likewise, the nations will rejoice in God after being revived (85.7)."

[72] *Ibid.*, 152.

Psalm 87 is the last Korahite psalm and speaks of God's love for Zion. It pinpoints Zion as the center of the future restoration. It strongly echoes Isaiah's imagery of Zion as mother: "For as soon as Zion was in labor she brought forth her sons" (Is. 66:8). The psalmist similarly describes the conversion of the nations at Mount Zion: "And of Zion it shall be said, 'This one and that one were born in her'"(Ps. 87:5). Here again we find the Psalter reflecting the hope of the prophets.

Psalm 88 is another psalm of an individual's lament, much like Davidic Psalm 86, but without a note of hope. This psalm leads to the dramatic plea of Psalm 89, in which the Davidic king seems to be vanquished, possibly even killed. The psalmist's last remaining hope is God's sworn covenant oath to David.

The King Cut Down

Psalm 89 begins by recalling God's covenant with David. In fact, nowhere does Scripture elaborate on God's oath to David in as much detail as is done here. The psalm recalls how the Davidic king was established as God's first-born, and how God promised that He would establish him "forever." Yet, the psalm goes on to explain the apparent failure of God's covenant. The psalmist indicts God saying, "Thou has renounced the covenant with thy servant; thou hast defiled his crown in the dust" (89:39). This reference to the crown "in the dust," along with the statement, "Thou hast cut short the days of his youth" (v. 45), seems to indicate the death of the king. The fact that the Hebrew word for "defiled" has a secondary meaning, "pierce," lends support to this interpretation.[73] In fact, a fatal "piercing" seems to be indicated: "[T]hou hast turned back the edge of his sword, and thou hast not made him stand in battle" (Ps. 89:43).

---

[73] Mitchell, *The Message of the Psalter*, 254.

For this reason, the psalm may be understood in the light of the prophetic books of Isaiah and Zechariah. Just as Psalm 89 speaks of David as the servant who is renounced (v. 39) and who bears the scorn and insults of the peoples, Isaiah prophesies about the suffering servant (Is. 53:11), who is "wounded for our transgressions" (Is. 53:5). He too is "despised and rejected" (Is. 53:3) and "bore the sin of many" (Is. 53:12), as the Davidic servant is "scorned" and "bears" the insults of the peoples (Ps. 89:50).

In like manner, Zechariah prophesies about a Davidic king who is "pierced" (Zech. 12:10). As in the lament of Psalm 89, the people of Israel "mourn" over him, and he is called the "first-born" (Zech. 12:10; cf. Ps. 89:27).

Yet, for both Isaiah and Zechariah the suffering servant of God will bring about the restoration of Israel. Isaiah goes on in chapter 54 to say: "For a brief moment I forsook you, but with great compassion I will gather you" (v. 7). He also speaks in chapter 55 of the restoration of the Davidic kingdom: "I will make with you an everlasting covenant, my steadfast, sure love for David. . . . Behold, you shall call nations that you know not, and nations that knew you not shall run to you" (vv. 3, 5). Themes from Psalm 89 appear in this brief passage, including a lasting covenant (Ps. 89:3, 28, 37) and God's steadfast love (Ps. 89:2, 24, 49).

Zechariah envisions a restoration of Israel following the coming of the "pierced" Davidic king as well. Whereas before Israel was "scattered" (Zech. 13:7), God will now call His people and they will return to Him: "They will call on my name, and I will answer them. I will say, 'They are my people'; and they will say, 'The LORD is my God'" (Zech. 13:9). This surely recalls the promise of Moses:

[T]hen the LORD your God will restore your fortunes, and have compassion upon you, and he will gather you again from all the peoples where the LORD your God has scattered you (Deut. 30:3).

Further, Psalm 89 confirms that David represents a kind of embodiment of Israel. David is called God's "first-born," much like Israel in Exodus 4:22. Likewise, David is made the "highest" of the kings of the earth, just as Israel is described as being "high above all the nations" in Deuteronomy 28:1.

Therefore, Book III, like Book II, portrays Israel's going into exile and their abiding hope in God on the basis of His covenant oath to David. As we saw earlier, this covenant is the climax of all the Old Testament covenants. For God to fail to honor His covenant with David would mean the failure of His oaths to Abraham, Israel, and even Adam. That is why Israel has confidence in the midst of affliction that the restoration will occur.[74] In fact, the whole of Book III can be seen in terms of alternating themes of lament and hope:

Theme	Psalm
Lament	73:1-13
Hope	**73:18-28**
Lament	74
Hope	**75; 76**
Lament	77:1-11
Hope	**77:12-21; 78**
Lament	79, 80
Hope	**81, 82**
Lament	83
Hope	**84**
Lament	85:1-8
Hope	**85:9-14**
Lament	86
Hope	**87**

---

[74] Israel also has the words of the prophets to reassure her, yet these remain secondary to the covenant.

Lament	88
Hope	**89:1-38**
Lament	89:39-52[75]

Book III, then, portrays Israel as exiled to the nations, and climaxes with the ultimate horror, the loss of the Davidic king.

BOOK IV (PSALMS 90-106)
Israel Deserted

Psalm 90, which begins Book IV, is the only psalm in the entire Psalter attributed to Moses. It is clearly a lament psalm and should probably be read in light of both the fall of the king in Psalm 89 as well as the larger context of going into exile. Here, then, we can see a hint of the hope of the New Exodus. Moses delivered Israel in the first Exodus, and now he is associated with the second.

Indeed, Psalms 90-100 all bear Mosaic/Exodus themes, serving as the prayer for restoration. Rabbinic tradition therefore recognized all of these psalms as Mosaic compositions, as Midrash I Psalm 90:3 demonstrates: "Moses composed eleven psalms appropriate to eleven tribes."[76] Origen, a third-century theologian, claimed to have learned this tradition from the Jews. Even so, the LXX ascribes Psalms 91 and 93-99 to David. Nevertheless, regardless of the attribution of these psalms, the prominent Exodus imagery is unmistakable.

Since it was Moses who reminded God that He could not destroy Israel without forsaking His covenant to Abraham (cf. Ex. 33), Moses' presence here may be understood in similar terms. In other words, God cannot forsake the covenant with David, which Psalm 89 asserts He has done, without violating the oaths He swore from of old. Furthermore, the Davidic

---

[75] McCann, "Books I-III and the Editorial Purpose of the Psalter," 97.
[76] Cited by Mitchell, *The Message of the Psalter*, 273.

kingdom may be hinted at by the use of the phrase "a thousand years" (Ps. 90:4), since this was an expression associated with it.[77] However, these references are rather obscure.

Psalm 90 begins by calling God Israel's "dwelling place" (v. 1). This description of God is found outside the Psalter only in Deuteronomy 33:27, underscoring the Mosaic tone of the psalm. Isaiah 8:14 uses similar imagery to describe a day when the Lord "will become a sanctuary." The image is also employed in Psalm 91:9.

Psalm 90 asks God for a "heart of wisdom" (v. 12). As we saw earlier, it was Moses who first instructed the people to follow the laws of the Lord in order to be wise. The connection of wisdom with a proper understanding of death is also made here, as Israel will become wise by knowing how to "number our days" (v. 12). So, Moses is portrayed as teaching Israel wisdom through its confrontation with death in the midst of exile. This is much like Psalm 78, which portrays the Israelites as repenting only when God slew them in the desert (v. 34). This evokes the image of Adam, who needed wisdom to overcome his fear of death, and David, who was guided by wisdom through his life-threatening ordeals.

Psalm 91, while not explicitly ascribed to Moses, seems to continue the imagery of an exodus. This is especially seen in vv. 11-12, where the psalmist assures his audience that God will send His angels "to guard you in all your ways . . . lest you dash your foot against a stone." Together with the imagery of the "lion," the "serpent," and the "adder" (v. 13), it is easy to read this passage as a depiction of God's continual guidance of His people in the wilderness. In fact, the only other time

---

[77] 2 Enoch 72:6: "And when the twelve generations shall come into being, and there will be one thousand and 70 years, and there will be born in that generation a righteous man . . . another Melkisedek." Charlesworth, *Old Testament Pseudepigrapha*, vol. 1, 210.

Scripture pairs together the adder and the serpent is in Deuteronomy 32:33.[78]

Just as Psalm 90 began with an echo of Deuteronomy 33, Psalm 91 also seems to draw heavily from Moses' final words in Deuteronomy, especially Moses' song in Deuteronomy 32:

Psalm 91	Deuteronomy 32
Lord is "the Most High" (v. 1)	Lord is "the Most High" (v. 8)
Lord is "refuge" and "fortress" (vv. 2, 9)	"they took refuge" (v. 37)
Lord covers Israel with "wings" and "pinions" (v. 4)	Lord is eagle who bears Israel "on its pinions" (v. 11)
"arrow that flies by day" (v. 5)	"spend my arrows upon them" (v. 23)
"deadly pestilence" (vv. 3, 6)	"poisonous pestilence" (v. 21)
surefootedness (v. 12)	"recompense for the time when their foot shall slip" (v. 35)

Spiritual Warfare

Psalm 91 also may be understood in terms of God's deliverance of Israel from demons. The "arrow that flies by day" (v. 6) may refer to a demonic archer. Resheph, a Canaanite god of pestilence, was also known as "Resheph of the arrow."[79] This would explain the close connection of "the arrow that flies by day" in v. 6 and the "pestilence" mentioned in v. 5. Support for this may be found in Deuteronomy 32:24, where Resheph is mentioned by name in the Hebrew.[80] Likewise, the "destruction that wastes at noonday" (v. 6) is rendered by the LXX as "the demon of noonday." Moreover, the "serpent" of

---

[78] These words may also be translated "dragon" and "venomous snake," thus perhaps evoking the imagery of Genesis 3. Mitchell, *The Message of the Psalter*, 278.
[79] *Ibid.*
[80] *Ibid.*

verse 13 is called δράκων or "dragon." This evokes Genesis 3, where the "serpent" is described as a "nahash," the seven-headed dragon Leviathan, and is later explicitly identified as the seven-headed "dragon" in Revelation 12:9.

The radical Essene community at Qumran also seems to have recognized Psalm 91 as referring to spiritual warfare, since the exorcism psalms in the Qumran collection include Psalm 91.[81] Likewise, rabbinic texts call the psalm "a song of the demons" or "song of demoniacs."[82] The connection of spiritual warfare with Psalm 91 is also made by the Liturgy of the Hours, which uses this psalm as part of Night Prayer (Compline) with the prayer: "Lord, we beg you to visit this house and banish from it all the deadly power of the enemy."

Psalm 92 has less explicit Song of Moses imagery than the preceding psalms. Yet, there are still some possible connections, which may explain why tradition has understood them in Mosaic terms.

Like the preceding psalm, the reference to the "Most High" (Ps. 92:1) recalls the Song of Moses. Psalm 92:15 describes the Lord as "my rock," as does Deuteronomy 32:4, 18, 30. The destruction of the wicked is also found in both passages (Ps. 92:9; Deut. 32:23-25). In addition, both speak of the "scattering" of evil-doers (Ps. 92:9; Deut. 32:26). Finally, the reference in Psalm 92:10 to God "exalting my horn like that of the wild ox" echoes the blessing of the tribe of Joseph in Deuteronomy 33:17.

Reigning Again

Psalms 93-100 exalt God as king over the nations. This too may call to mind Exodus imagery, since the song Israel sang after passing through the Red Sea, referred to as the Song of the Sea, describes the Lord as "reigning" (Ex. 15:18). Hence,

---

[81] *Ibid.*, 279.
[82] *Ibid.*

after Psalm 93:1 proclaims "the LORD reigns," the psalmist speaks of the "floodwaters" and the "sea" (vv. 3-4).

Psalm 94 beautifully illustrates what we have said from the beginning about suffering as God's fatherly discipline. The psalmist explains: "Blessed is the man whom thou dost chasten, O Lord, and whom thou dost teach out of thy law" (v. 12). Likewise, God teaches all the nations (v. 10). The psalm does not seem to have much in the way of Mosaic imagery. However, the psalm's continual use of the Lord as "rock" and "refuge" may tie it to the Exodus themes of the previous psalms.

Psalm 95 draws heavily from Israel's wilderness experience. Its opening reference to singing to the Lord God, described as the "Rock," evokes Deuteronomy 32, like other psalms in this section. Its call to praise God and its declaration, "For the LORD is a great God" (v. 3) evokes the opening of Moses' song: "Ascribe greatness to our God!" (Deut. 32:3). The psalm also evokes the sea imagery of Exodus 15: "The sea is his, for he made it" (v. 5).

Psalm 95 ends with the recollection of Israel's disobedience in Exodus 17. This is noteworthy in two respects. First, this event occurs on the heels of God's miraculous parting of the Red Sea. Second, this warning against disobedience is also recorded in Deuteronomy 33:8, so the psalm must also be connected to that context. This psalm, therefore, brings together the two recurring contexts alluded to in Psalms 90-100. Set in the context of the exile, Psalm 95 calls upon Israel in the wilderness of the nations not to forget the works God has wrought in the past, while at the same time nurturing the hope of a future miraculous deliverance.

Psalms 96-99 continue in the same vein as the previous psalms. They also evoke the Song of Moses and the Song of the Sea with their invitations to "sing to the LORD a new song" (96:1; 98:1). Mitchell observes: "[T]his time a *new song* is to be sung, suggesting a new order of redemption, comparable with the redemption from Egypt, but greater."[83]

References to the glory-cloud of the Lord, which guided Israel through the desert, are also found in these psalms. For example, we read: "Clouds and thick darkness are round about him; righteousness and justice are the foundation of his throne. Fire goes before him, and burns up his adversaries round about" (Ps. 97:2-3). Psalm 99 also remembers how the Lord "spoke to them in the pillar of cloud" (99:7). These two psalms place God's reign in the context of Zion (Ps. 97:8; 99:1). Hence, God's reign is still linked with the "city of David," even if the Davidic king has temporarily been removed.

If we step back, we can see how these four psalms form an interlocking unit, divided into the psalms which represent "a new song to the Lord"—containing references to the Lord's parting of the sea—and psalms of Yahweh reigning, which is linked with Zion imagery.

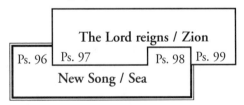

Further, by combining Zion with Exodus imagery, the reader gets a picture very similar to Isaiah 40-66.

Isaiah 40-66 depicts Exodus imagery as it describes the New Exodus. There the Lord promises to gather back Israel to Himself (49:5). He will bring them to Mount Zion (51:3; 51:10; 59:20), where God will "reign" (52:7) with the Davidic king (55:3-5) over all the nations (45:22; 60:3; 66:20). The passage begins with Exodus imagery: "A voice cries: 'In the wilderness prepare the way of the LORD, make straight in the

---

[83] *Ibid.*, 288 (original emphasis).

desert a highway for our God" (40:3). These are all motifs found in Psalms 90-100.

Many other images that appear in Psalms 90-100 are also found in Isaiah 40-66. Isaiah 42:10 could easily have been the source for some of the psalms in this section: "Sing to the LORD a new song, his praise from the end of the earth! Let the sea roar and all that fills it. . . ." Other themes include the Lord as "rock" (44:8) and the Lord as "refuge" (57:13). With all these connections in mind, it is surely no stretch to see Psalms 90-100 as referring to the same New Exodus prophesied by Isaiah.

Psalm 100 brings this section to a climax. The super-scription reads "A Psalm for the thank offering." Clearly, given the context of Israel's exilic ordeal, the psalm is meant to function as kind of corporate *todah*, even though this was not an offering specified by the Mosaic law. Nonetheless, just as David offered his suffering up in thanksgiving, Israel is pre-sented as following his example.

A Ray of Hope

Psalm 101 is a Davidic psalm and seems to reveal the first glimmer of hope for a Davidic king since Psalm 89. The psalmist states: "Oh when wilt thou come to me? I will walk with integrity of heart within my house" (v. 2). Thus, the king seems to be preparing himself to once again take his throne. He goes on to plan his campaign to vindicate God's people: "Morning by morning I will destroy all the wicked in the land, cutting off all the evildoers from the city of the LORD" (v. 8).

Psalm 102 then announces that "the appointed time has come," that God will look favorably on Israel (v. 13). This verse brings to mind Psalm 75:2: "At the set time which I appoint I will judge with equity." Psalm 102 announces that the Lord has looked down from heaven "to hear the groans of the prisoners, to set free those who were doomed to die"

(v. 20)—a reference to the setting free of those held captive in the exile. Therefore, the time has come that the Lord will have pity on Zion, so that "peoples gather together, and kingdoms, to worship the LORD" (v. 22).

Almost as a response to the announcement that the appointed time has come, Psalm 103 is another psalm attributed to David in which he blesses the Lord. The psalm depicts the redemption of God, blessing the One "who redeems your life from the Pit, who crowns you with steadfast love and mercy" (v. 4). The language here also clearly echoes Psalm 89, where the Davidic king wondered if God's steadfast love had come to an end (v. 49), as his "crown" was defiled in the dust and his life threatened and perhaps even taken (vv. 38-45). Likewise, while Psalm 89 said, "thou has cut short the days of his youth" (v. 45), Psalm 103 reports: "your youth is renewed like the eagle's" (v. 5). The psalm begins and ends with the recurring theme of "Bless the LORD, O my soul" (103:1, 20-22), praising God for restoring His kingdom (v. 19).

Psalms 104-106 then proceed to summarize salvation history. Psalm 104 recounts God's creation of the world and is framed the same way Psalm 103 is, "Bless the LORD, O my soul" (104:1, 35). The psalm then concludes: "Praise the LORD!" (v. 35). Psalm 105 recalls the lives of the patriarchs and Moses, ending as Psalm 104 did, "Praise the LORD!" (v. 45). Finally, Book IV concludes with a psalm that tells more about Israel's wandering in the wilderness, ending with the plea to "gather us from among the nations, that we may give thanks to thy holy name and glory in thy praise" (106:47). Psalm 106 also begins and ends with the same recurring phrase as Psalms 104 and 105, "Praise the LORD!" (v. 48).

The cumulative effect of these three psalms is to present the restoration of Israel from exile under the Davidic king as the fulfillment of all salvation history. By bringing mankind back

to Himself through the son of David and the kingdom of
God, the Lord accomplishes His goal in creation, fulfills His
oath to Abraham, realizes the vocation of Israel, and remembers
the covenant He swore to David.

BOOK V (PSALMS 107-50)
Kingdom Come

Book V may be divided up into three major parts:
Psalms 107-19; 120-36; and 137-50. As we shall see, each
of these sections seems to depict a cycle of restoration.
Each section also concludes with a psalm or psalms of
"Praise the LORD!"

Book IV stated that the purpose of the restoration is to
"gather us from among the nations, that we may give thanks
to thy holy name and glory in thy praise" (Ps. 106:47). This is
also the theme at the outset of Book V. Psalm 107 begins by
depicting the "thanks" (v. 1) offered to God by those "gathered
in from the lands" (v. 3). Just as Moses had foretold in
Deuteronomy 30 and David had prayed in Psalm 86:7, Israel
in exile "cried to the LORD in their trouble, and he delivered
them from their distress" (v. 6). The psalmist then declares:
"Let them thank the LORD" (v. 8). This pattern of "they cried
to the LORD . . . and he delivered them . . . let them thank
the LORD" recurs throughout the psalm as a kind of refrain
(vv. 6-8, 13-15, 19-22, 28-31).

Furthermore, it is clear that this thanksgiving is a *todah*
sacrifice: "And let them offer sacrifices of thanksgiving" (v. 22).
Here we see that the *todah* is the appropriate offering of
restored Israel. Whoever does this, the psalmist tells us, is
"wise" (v. 43).

Yet, Psalms 108-09 depict Israel still struggling against its
enemies. It seems, then, that the restoration has begun but is
still incomplete. Psalm 108 describes one who is steadfast in
his ordeal, promising to give thanks—almost as if he had

taken heed of the instruction of Psalm 107. Likewise, Psalm 109 asks God to bring down the wicked. The stage is now set for the ultimate vindication of the Davidic king.

The Empire Strikes Back

Psalm 110 was probably an enthronement psalm of the Davidic king.[84] The superscription attributes the psalm to David, who may have sung this psalm on the day of Solomon's enthronement. Since David himself referred to King Saul as "my Lord,"[85] there is no problem in seeing the opening statement, "The LORD says to my lord," as an address to his newly enthroned son. This is made even more likely by the fact that David made his son king while he was still alive (cf. 1 Kings 1:29-48).

However, within the larger context of the exile experience and the affliction of Israel in the preceding psalms, Psalm 110 represents the triumphant return of the Davidic king. With this messianic enthronement, the hope for the restoration of the kingdom can finally be realized. In response to the laments of Psalms 108-09, which spoke of the continued affliction of the righteous by the wicked, Psalm 110 proclaims: "Sit at my right hand, till I make your enemies your footstool."

As always, this restoration takes place on Zion (v. 2). There the people will "offer themselves freely" (v. 3). Thus, Adam's original calling to offer life-giving love will finally be fulfilled

---

[84] Mays, *Psalms*, 351: "The first divine saying (v. 1) is an instruction to assume the throne, and the whole was probably composed to be used in inaugural ceremonies for the king at the point of his enthronement. The psalm, then, served as a text for the installation of a king in office." See also Eaton, *Kingship and the Psalms*, 124.

[85] Hahn, *Kinship by Covenant*, 330-31: "The question is, who would David call 'my lord' in addressing this oracle from Yahweh? Earlier in his lifetime, David used 'my lord' with reference to King Saul (1 Sam. 24:6-10; 26:17-19) and Achish, the Philistine king (1 Sam. 29:8), even after Samuel had anointed David as king (1 Sam. 16:11-13). Such an expression was used by David, then, in addressing kings, though neither Saul nor Achish qualify as likely candidates for Psalm 110:1. The only other royal candidate in David's lifetime would have been Solomon."

by God's people on Zion. Humanity will at last enter into the "self-giving" life of the Trinity there in the restored Jerusalem.

Psalms 111-13 are a response of praise in light of this restored kingdom. The psalms are framed by the phrase "Praise the LORD!" which begins Psalms 111 and 112, and frames 113. Unlike the concern that God had abandoned His covenant in Psalm 89, Psalm 111 states: "[H]e is ever mindful of his covenant."

Psalms 114-18 are sung during the Passover seder and are known as the "great hallel."[86] Psalm 116 is particularly interesting because it depicts the offering of the *todah*: "I will offer to thee the sacrifice of thanksgiving" (v. 17). In addition, Psalm 118 concludes the section, proclaiming, "O give thanks to the LORD, for he is good; for his steadfast love endures for ever!" (v. 29).

Psalm 119 is the longest psalm in the Psalter. It is an acrostic psalm, meaning that each line of the Psalm begins with successive letters in the Hebrew alphabet. This made it easier to memorize the psalm.

This psalm, with its prominent wisdom themes, is related to Psalm 1. The opening statement, "Blessed are those whose way is blameless, who walk in the law of the LORD" (v. 1), immediately evokes Psalm 1:1. There we read about the blessed man who "walks not in the counsel of the wicked" but whose "delight is in the law of the LORD" (Ps. 1:1-2). Psalm 119:15 says, "I will meditate on thy precepts" as the man in Psalm 1:2 "meditates" on the law. It thus seems that Psalm 119 stretches back to the beginning of the Psalter, bringing out and summarizing the lessons of the various psalms.

An example of this would be the psalm's understanding of affliction. Psalm 119 portrays suffering as the means by which one truly comes to learn God's statutes: "It is good for me that

---

[86] Joachim Jeremias, *The Eucharistic Words of Jesus* (London: SCM Press, 1960), 55, 86.

I was afflicted, that I might learn thy statutes" (v. 71). Furthermore, through proper fear—fear of the Lord—one endures affliction righteously, trusting in the Lord to bring deliverance: "Those who fear thee shall see me and rejoice, because I have hoped in thy word" (Ps. 119:74).

The Ascent of Faith

At the end of Psalm 119, the psalmist appears to be back in a situation of affliction. This sets up the Ascent psalms, which again recount the restoration. The Ascent psalms stand at the center of Book V. It appears that these fifteen psalms were originally sung as worshippers ascended the fifteen steps of the Temple.[87] However, these psalms also seem to describe the restoration, and thus summarize the movement of the whole Psalter. Mitchell explains the progression of these psalms as follows.

The psalmist of 120 appears to be in exile: "Too long have I had my dwelling among those who hate peace" (v. 6). This is followed by what appears to be a song of pilgrimage to Zion. In it the psalmist appears to be assured of God's protection as he returns to Jerusalem.[88] Then Psalm 122 announces the arrival of the psalmist in Jerusalem: "Our feet have been standing within your gates, O Jerusalem" (v. 2).

Next, the psalmist in Psalm 123 prays for mercy upon Israel, thus indicating that Israel is still persecuted by its neighbors: "Too long our soul has been sated with the scorn of those who are at ease, the contempt of the proud" (v. 4). In other words, as in the period before David, Israel had entered the land but not yet received "rest" from her enemies. Next, Psalm 124 offers thanksgiving—much like Psalm 108.

---

[87] Mitchell, *The Message of the Psalter*, 109.

[88] *Ibid.*, 118: "The pilgrim traveling upward through the Judean foothills raises his eyes to the mountains of Zion and affirms that his helper on pilgrimage is Yhwh (vv. 102). It is he who keeps from stumbling on the road, shades from burning sun and baleful moon, protects from all harm and guards his coming and going."

Again, following the example of David, Israel continues to offer *todah* in the midst of affliction.

Psalm 125 explains that the Lord will continue to protect Jerusalem. Yet, Psalm 126:4 states, "Restore our fortunes, O LORD," indicating that the restoration is not yet complete. Hence, in Psalm 127 the rebuilding of the Temple is depicted: "Unless the LORD builds the house, those who build it labor in vain" (v. 1). In other words, the rebuilding of Jerusalem must be undertaken with the blessing of God. Interestingly, it is ascribed to Solomon, who built the first Temple. Psalm 128, therefore, shows the way to this blessing: "Blessed is every one who fears the LORD, who walks in his ways!" (v. 1).

Psalm 129 recalls the affliction of the exile, but minimizes it. The psalmist recalls the suffering of long ago—the suffering of his youth (v. 1). Psalm 130 then reveals the true heart of the problem of exile: *sin*. Though Israel's temporal enemies have been routed, the people still must be freed from sin. Thus, for the first time in the Ascent psalms, the psalmist prays that the Lord will "redeem Israel from all its iniquities," not just its suffering (v. 8). This leads to the humble prayer of Psalm 131, which deals with interior peace. The psalm ends by instructing Israel to continue to hope in the Lord.

Like Psalm 110, Psalm 132 marks the capstone of the restoration by recounting the coming of the Lord and the Davidic king to Zion. The close connection of their comings reveals that only in the restoration of the Davidic kingdom will God finally restore His people to Himself. David has finally achieved "rest" from Israel's enemies. Indeed, this psalm seems to have its origin in the bringing up of the ark to Jerusalem, after David had achieved "rest" by conquering Zion. This psalm was discussed in detail earlier in our discussion of the Davidic covenant.[89]

---

[89] See pp. 54-55, *supra.*

Following the return of the Davidic king to Zion in Psalm 132, Psalm 133 envisions a restoration of all Israel: "Behold, how good and pleasant it is when brothers dwell in unity" (v. 1). Psalm 134 concludes the Ascent psalms. The first part of the psalm represents the people exhorting the priests who minister in the Temple of God: "Come, bless the LORD, all you servants of the LORD, who stand by night in the house of the LORD!" (v. 1). The last verse of this short psalm then appears to be the concluding blessing by the priests of the people: "May the LORD bless you from Zion, he who made heaven and earth!" (v. 3). Therefore, after the Davidic king returns to Zion, Israel's struggle with her enemies comes to an end—"rest" has been achieved. The final Ascent psalms portray Israel reunited, living in peace.

Clearly the Ascent psalms begin with Israel in exile and climax in the restoration. Mitchell's observation of movement from Psalm 120, where the psalmist dwells in a foreign country, to Psalms 133-34, where Israel dwells together in unity on Zion, is certainly representative of the text itself. Further, the connection of the Lord drawing Israel to Zion and the establishment of the Davidic king is clearly discernable.

Praise the Lord!

Psalms 135-36, proceed to offer extensive "praise" and "thanksgiving," reminiscent of the praise found in Psalms 111-13 and the thanksgiving offered in Psalm 107. Psalm 135 is framed with the same "Praise the LORD," which begins and ends Psalms 111-13. Likewise, Psalm 136, which recalls God's merciful deliverance in times past, begins the same way Psalm 107 does, "O give thanks to the LORD, for he is good" and concludes with a similar offering of thanks.

Psalm 137 stands out strikingly from the other psalms of Book V. This psalm depicts Israel still in exile, hoping to return to Zion. Following it, Psalms 138-43 contain another collection of Davidic lament psalms. Like the other Davidic collections, *todah* is here offered by the psalmist as he prays for deliverance: "I give thee thanks, O LORD, with my heart" (Ps. 138:1).

Psalm 144 anticipates the victory of the Davidic king: "I will sing a new song to thee, O God . . . who rescuest David thy servant" (vv. 9-10). Psalm 145 then describes a restored kingdom: "Thy kingdom is an everlasting kingdom, and thy dominion endures throughout all generations" (v. 13). Although it is not specified that this kingdom is the Davidic kingdom, God's kingdom and the Davidic kingdom are combined by the Psalter (and by other canonical books, such as Chronicles) so that no real dichotomy exists between the two.

Psalms 146-50 go on to offer "praise" much like the psalms after the restoration (Psalms 11-13) and the praise psalm following the Ascents (Ps. 135). In all three instances, psalms that depict the vindication of the Davidic king and the restoration of the kingdom are followed by a series of psalms framed by "Praise the LORD!"

Book V, then, depicts the restoration and celebrates as Psalm 106 (which ends Book IV), describes: "that we may give *thanks* to thy holy name and glory in thy *praise*" (v. 47). Book V frames the description of the New Exodus and the gathering of Israel under the Davidic king by psalms of *thanks* (107) and *praise* (147-50). Of course, it is impossible to say with certainty whether this was actually the intent of the editor(s) of the Psalter. Nevertheless, Book V does emphasize the theme of final restoration by describing it in three separate cycles, which are each then followed by psalms of "Praise the LORD!"

Layers of Meaning

The Book of Psalms must be read at three levels. First, each of the psalms must be read as individual prayers, which stand on their own, apart from their context. Second, many of these psalms may be understood as composed for some specific historical context, such as Psalm 110 as the enthronement of the king, and Psalm 132 as the bringing up of the ark to Jerusalem. Finally, the psalms gain new meaning as they are placed in the larger context of the Psalter. Such is the case with Psalm 90 which, as a response to Psalm 89, becomes emblematic of the hope of the New Exodus.[90]

Further, the Psalms bring together the experience of David and Israel—the first-born of God. David serves as a kind of example for Israel in its affliction. He embodies the wise man who endures suffering by learning to offer *todah*, trusting in the Lord. More than he fears death, he fears the Lord, who will ultimately deliver him from his suffering.

The Psalter is thus permeated by the hope for the restoration of the Davidic kingdom where all twelve tribes, even the northern ones scattered to the nations, will return and bring the nations to worship the Lord on Zion. There, Israel will enter into the Lord's presence, as He will become their "refuge" and "dwelling place." This hope is all predicated upon God's covenant oath, which He swore to David, through which all previous covenants will be fulfilled. The Psalter's expression of hope is confirmed by the reading of the individual psalms and is underscored by the arrangement of the Psalter as a whole.

---

[90] Similarly, Schaper explains how Psalm 69, which originally recounts Israel's deliverance from Egypt, is recast in the light of the hope for the New Exodus: "What used to be, in the Hebrew, a praise of God's work in Israelite history has been partly transformed into an announcement of his eschatological actions." *Eschatology in the Greek Psalter*, 86.

PART II

JESUS AND THE RESTORATION OF THE KINGDOM

✡ CHAPTER 5 ✡

RESTORING ALL THINGS
IN CHRIST

The kingdom of David represented the partial fulfillment of all the Old Testament covenants. Through the Davidic covenant, God's promise to restore all mankind to Himself would be realized. The primary purpose of the kingdom was not to amass great wealth or impressive military power, but rather to unite all men with God on Mount Zion.

The restoration of the kingdom has implications for all previous Old Testament covenants. If God failed to restore the kingdom of David, all Old Testament covenant promises would be left unfulfilled. The restoration of the kingdom is therefore inseparably linked to the restoration of the original Adamic state, the keeping of the Abrahamic covenant, and the realization of Israel's calling as God's first-born son among the nations. Jesus Christ, the Son of God, perfectly fulfilled each of these covenants. Here's how.

Adam

Adam failed to satisfy the requirements of the covenant because he failed to offer his life as a priestly sacrifice to God in the garden. His fear of death prevented Him from loving God more than his own life. Adam's failure triggered the covenant curses. These curses included nakedness, sweat, his work bearing thorns instead of fruit, and death (cf. Gen. 3:7, 18-19). In order to restore the covenant, these curses needed to be borne redemptively.

Adam's sin indicted all humanity. Because of this, no man, however just, would be exempt from the covenant curses. Man now not only owed God complete and total life-giving love—since this was Adam's vocation from the beginning—but he also had to bear the curses of the covenant. Therefore, the only way the demands of the covenant could be satisfied would be for God to become man and bear the curses redemptively, as a man not under the curse.[1]

The New Covenant remedies Adam's covenant-breaking in Christ, who bears the curses of mankind. Hahn explains:

> As the new Adam, Jesus was tested in the garden, where "his sweat became like great drops of blood." Jesus then had a "crown of thorns" placed upon his head, before he was taken to the "tree," where he was stripped naked. Then he fell into the deep sleep of death, so that from his side would come forth the New Eve.[2]

The New Covenant, then, restores the divine sonship that was lost by Adam. We are able to once again enjoy interpersonal communion with God.

In this, the *theologia* sheds light on the *oikonomia*.[3] Earlier, we saw that the Son is truly the image of the Father because He returns the Father's self-donating love by pouring out His own life. Adam was likewise called to life-giving love by virtue of the divine sonship God had bestowed upon him. Adam

---

[1] See Anselm, *Cur Deus Homo?* (Why the God Man?). Saint Anselm explained that man owed God everything by his very creation. Hence, once man fell into sin, he incurred a debt he could never pay, since he already owed everything to God. Thus, God became man so "satisfaction" could be paid. Many theologians explain this simply in terms of feudal society, where a serf owed his master honor. A richer, Trinitarian understanding would view this as man owing God life-giving love through filial charity.

[2] Scott Hahn, *A Father Who Keeps His Promises*, 75 (citations omitted).

[3] Recall that the *theologia* is who God is, while the *oikonomia* explains what God does in history.

needed to mature in his sonship—realize it, so to speak—by offering his own life out of love. This is because sonship involves pouring back one's life in love.

Suffering, therefore, is not an arbitrary test. God does not call those in covenant with Him to suffer simply because He wishes to balance the scales of pleasure and pain. God does not say to man: "I will let you enjoy happiness forever in heaven, but only if you suffer for a while on earth." Instead, Christ's death and suffering in general must be understood as the fullest expression of life-giving love (cf. Jn. 15:13).

When Jesus suffered and died on the Cross, He revealed in history what He does from all eternity—that is, He pours Himself out in life-giving love to the Father, through the Spirit. In other words, Christ's suffering on the Cross is the historical manifestation of His eternal act of love in the life of the Trinity. God does in time what He does from all eternity.

Further, we see that the covenant curse of death triggered by Adam was no more arbitrary than the ordeal. Death is the means by which man can irrevocably offer God the gift of his life. In death, man presents his life as a sacrificial gift—death is the ultimate expression of life-giving love.[4] Hence, Christ fulfills the demands of the Adamic covenant. He is the true High Priest who offers Himself as the perfect victim.

---

[4] Martin Foss, *Death, Sacrifice, and Tragedy* (Lincoln, NE: University of Nebraska Press, 1966), 74: "When sacrifice entered the scene, a light broke through the darkness; absurdity gave way to meaning, and life was rediscovered when used as a gracious gift, a precious offering." Likewise, Hans Urs von Balthasar writes: "When the Father surrenders himself unreservedly to the Son, and when, in turn, the Father and Son surrender themselves similarly to the Holy Spirit, do we not find here the archetype of the most beautiful dying in the midst of eternal life? Is this final state of 'not wanting to be for oneself' not precisely the prerequisite for the most blessed life? Into this most living 'higher dying' our own wretched dying is taken up and resolved, so that everything human . . . is thenceforth securely integrated into a life that no longer knows any limits." *Credo: Meditations on the Apostles' Creed* (New York: Crossroad Publishing, 1990), 59.

Abraham

The next figure we looked at in salvation history was
Abraham, who received three promises in Genesis 12, which
were strengthened by covenant oaths in chapters 15, 17, and 22.
In Genesis 15, Abram is promised that his descendants will
be a great nation. This is fulfilled in Israel. In Genesis 17,
God swears that kings will come from his descendants,
which is realized in the Davidic covenant. Finally, in Genesis
22, God commands Abraham to offer Isaac, his only beloved
son, as a sacrifice. After God sees that Abraham is willing to
comply, God stops Abraham, swearing to bless all nations
through his descendants.

While Genesis 22 is partially fulfilled by the Davidic
kingdom, which included Gentiles, Jesus fulfills this covenant
oath perfectly in His self-offering on the Cross. The sacrifice
of Christ is prefigured in both Abraham and Isaac. First,
Abraham foreshadows God the Father who offers His only
beloved Son. Thus, we read from Saint Irenaeus:

> In fact, in Abraham mankind has learned and become accus-
> tomed to following the Word of God, voluntarily giving the
> sacrifice of his only son, his beloved son, so that God might
> be pleased to make the sacrifice of His only Son, His beloved,
> for all his descendants indeed, for our redemption.[5]

Second, since Isaac may be understood as a willing victim,[6]
he may be understood as a type of Christ, who freely offered
Himself in sacrifice. Saint Clement of Alexandria wrote:

---

[5] *Against Heresies*, Book IV, chapter 5, no. 4, as quoted in Mieczyslaw Paczkowski,
"The Sacrifice of Isaac in Early Patristic Exegesis," *The Sacrifice of Isaac in the Three
Monotheistic Religions*, Frederic Manns, ed. (Jerusalem: Franciscan Printing Press,
1995), 106.
[6] See p. 48, *supra*.

Isaac . . . is a type of the Lord . . . He was a child, just as the
Son . . . for he was the son of Abraham, as Christ is the Son
of God. He was a sacrificial victim, as was the Lord.[7]

Many other elements of the story may also be understood
as pointing to Christ. Isaac carried the wood of the sacrifice on
his back as he walked up the mountain, just as Christ later
carried the Cross up the road to Calvary. The place where
Abraham offered Isaac is Mount Moriah, the same mountain
range upon which Golgotha stands. Abraham received his son
back from under the curse of death on the third day, the same
day Christ was raised.[8]

Moreover, Abraham told Isaac that "God will provide
himself the lamb" (Gen. 22:8). This prophecy was fulfilled in
Christ, the Lamb of God. As we saw earlier, the cult of the
Temple served as a kind of substitutionary sacrifice, which
reminded God of His promise to Abraham. Christ's sacrificial
offering abolished this cult, because it fulfilled the promise.

By fulfilling the covenant promise of Genesis 22, Jesus
makes it possible for all men to be blessed, thus fulfilling
God's promise to Abraham. Thus, Saint Paul states that Christ
died so that "the blessing of Abraham might come upon the
Gentiles, that we might receive the promise of the Spirit
through faith" (Gal. 3:14). While Abraham partially reversed
the curses incurred by Adam, Jesus reverses them *completely*.

Israel

Finally, the covenant curses incurred by Israel's worship of
the golden calf are also borne redemptively by Christ. Israel
had rightly deserved to be destroyed for breaking the covenant

---

[7] *The Instructor*, Book I, chapter 5, as quoted in Paczkowski, "The Sacrifice of Isaac
in Early Patristic Exegesis," 110.

[8] Jean Danielou, *From Shadows to Reality*, Wulston Hibbard, trans. (Westminster,
MD: The Newman Press, 1960), 130.

they had entered into with God. Yet, Israel was spared because of God's oath to Abraham. Israel was given a lower law, the ceremonial law of Deuteronomy, which was meant to make them realize their sinfulness. This law quarantined them from the nations and prevented them from going out and converting the nations.

Saint Paul shows how Christ bore the covenant curse incurred by Israel by hanging on a tree (cf. Gal. 3:13). Deuteronomy states that anyone who "hangs on a tree" is cursed (21:22). Christ therefore bears the curse redemptively, dying the death Israel made necessary through its breaking the covenant. The curse is borne without God's having to break His covenant promise to Abraham.[9]

In all of this, Christ fulfills the demands of the Old Testament covenants. In this light, the New Covenant is not "new" because it is "novel." Rather, it is the realization of God's plan from the beginning of history.

---

[9] Hahn, *Kinship by Covenant*, 489: "[A]s the anointed representative for Israel and the nations, Christ dies on the cross in order to bear the curses of the broken (Deuteronomic) covenant—in accord with God's covenant oath to Abraham at the Aqedah." Hahn also shows how the animal sacrifices of the Levites were only temporary substitutes for an inevitable curse-bearing death: "[W]ith the breaking of the ('first') covenant, Israel's death becomes legally necessary because of the curses which were attendant to the oath, as signified by the sacrifice. . . . Christ thus fulfills the covenant not only by bearing the curse-of-death but by doing so as a faithful firstborn son of God and royal high priest, thereby fulfilling the vocation that Israel first accepted (Ex. 19-24)." *Ibid.*, 614-15.

✡ CHAPTER 6 ✡

JESUS AND THE RESTORATION OF THE KINGDOM

A Dream Come True

The hope for the restoration of the kingdom of David with the nations on Mount Zion is exactly what the New Testament writers understood Christ as fulfilling. Although this theme can be found in almost all of the twenty-seven New Testament books, we will limit our analysis to the study of the Gospel of Matthew. We have chosen this book because Matthew is the Gospel that most clearly demonstrates Jesus' interest in the kingdom.[1]

The Gospel of Matthew begins with a genealogy, identifying Jesus as the "son of David, the son of Abraham" (Mt. 1:1). Therefore, from the outset, Jesus is linked with the two figures in salvation history through whom God swore to bless all the nations (cf. Gen. 22:18; Ps. 72:17). The genealogy in its entirety has a strong Davidic note, dividing itself up into three sets of fourteen generations. This is significant because David's name appears in Hebrew the same way the number "fourteen" is written.[2] It is also interesting that the genealogy does not mention the return from exile, even though many of the Jews had already returned from Babylon. This indicates that the true New Exodus has not yet occurred.

---

[1] Edward P. Sri, *Mystery of the Kingdom: On the Gospel of Matthew* (Steubenville, OH: Emmaus Road Publishing, 1999), 15: "Matthew, more than the other Gospels, brings together most explicitly this central theme of Jesus' mission, the building of the kingdom."

[2] *Ibid.*, 21.

Matthew 2 mentions two cities with Davidic connections. First, we read that Jesus is born in Bethlehem, the city of David (cf. 1 Sam. 17:12). Later, Saint Matthew tells us that the Holy Family settled in the town of Nazareth to fulfill a prophecy: "He shall be called a Nazarene" (Mt. 2:23). Yet, there is no prophecy in the Old Testament that states such a thing. Matthew is apparently drawing on the association of the word "Nazarene" to the Hebrew word *netser*, which is translated "branch."[3] This association brings many prophecies into play.

One example of a "branch" prophecy is Isaiah 11:1. Since Matthew cites Isaiah frequently, it is likely that he had this text in mind. God promises in this passage that "[t]here shall come forth a shoot from the stump of Jesse, and a branch shall grow out of his roots" (Is. 11:1). Jesse was David's father. When the Davidic king was killed and Israel went into exile, it appeared that the family tree of David had been cut down. Yet, God promised that a branch would grow from "the stump," indicating the hope of a Davidic king who would restore the kingdom. There are many other "branch" prophecies in the Old Testament that reflect the same hope.[4]

Matthew 2 also cites a prophecy from Hosea, which refers to the return of the tribes in captivity. Matthew quotes Hosea 11:1, but let us look at it in the larger context of the chapter. Hosea 11 recounts how God brought Israel up out of Egypt (v. 1). The passage goes on, however, to speak of Israel's rebellion against God (v. 2). Because of its sin, God delivered Israel over to the nations in the exile: "They shall return to the land of Egypt, and Assyria shall be their king, because they have

---

[3] Scott Hahn and Curtis Mitch, eds., *Ignatius Study Bible: The Gospel of Matthew* (San Francisco: Ignatius Press, 2000), 21.
[4] For example, Zechariah 3:8-9 states: "I will bring my servant the Branch . . . and I will remove the guilt of this land in a single day."

refused to return to me" (v. 5). Yet, God promises that He will return them from the lands to which they have been scattered:

> They shall go after the LORD . . . and his sons shall come trembling from the west; they shall come trembling like birds from Egypt, and like doves from the land of Assyria; and I will return them to their homes (vv. 10-11).

Matthew applies the first verse of this prophecy to Jesus, who left Egypt, where He was hiding from Herod, and moved to Nazareth: "[O]ut of Egypt I called my son" (Hos. 11:1; Mt. 2:15). Just as the Davidic king embodied the experience of Israel, so too does Jesus.

In Matthew 3:2, John the Baptist makes his appearance, preaching that "the kingdom of heaven is at hand." John's presence calls to mind the New Exodus prophecy in Isaiah 40: "The voice of one crying in the wilderness: Prepare the way of the Lord" (Mt. 3:3). As if this were not enough of an indication that John perceived himself as announcing the restoration, we also read that he wore a garment of "camel's hair" and a "leather girdle." This was the attire of Elijah (cf. 2 Kings 1:8), who we are told in Sirach will come "at the appointed time . . . to restore the tribes of Jacob" (Sir. 48:10).

In Matthew 4, Jesus begins His ministry at Capernaum, a town located at the intersection of the ancient tribal territories of Zebulun and Naphtali.[5] This, we are told, fulfilled what Isaiah prophesied: "The land of Zebulun and the land of Naphtali, toward the sea, across the Jordan, Galilee of the Gentiles . . . have seen a great light" (Mt. 4:15-16; cf. Is. 9:1-2). Galilee was the northern part of Israel, which had fallen prey to Assyria's first campaign in 733-32 B.C. However, unlike the tribes in the heart of the northern kingdom, which were all

---

[5] Hahn and Mitch, *The Gospel of Matthew*, 23.

scattered to the nations, many Israelites from this region remained behind after the invasion. For this reason, the Galileans were often recognized as true Israelites.

Jesus therefore goes to these Israelites up north to fulfill Isaiah's prophecy. In other words, the restoration of the kingdom begins where the deportation began. Jesus is concerned with restoring a Pan-Israelite kingdom, which includes the Judeans down south, and the Galileans up north.[6] In fact, once Jesus arrives, His message is: "Repent, for the kingdom of heaven is at hand" (Mt. 4:17).[7] We are told that He went all over Galilee preaching "the gospel of the kingdom" (Mt. 4:23).[8]

Family of God

Jesus refers to the "kingdom" several times in His Sermon on the Mount, recorded in Matthew 5-7. Indeed, the Beatitudes begin, "Blessed are the poor in spirit, for theirs is the *kingdom* of heaven" (Mt. 5:3). This section of Matthew also has a high concentration of familial imagery. In fact, before

---

[6] Freyne shows how Jesus' ministry in Galilee may be understood in terms of Israel's hope for the restored kingdom. Sean Freyne, *Galilee, Jesus and the Gospels: Literary Approaches and Historical Investigations* (Philadelphia: Fortress Press, 1988), 266-67.

[7] Repentance is often linked with restoration. For example, David's penitential prayer in Psalm 51 includes a petition to rebuild the walls of Jerusalem (v. 18). Hence, we should not be surprised to see "repentance" and the imagery of the "kingdom" frequently paired. Blaine Charette, *Restoring Presence: The Spirit in Matthew's Gospel* (Sheffield, England: Sheffield Academic Press, 2000), 44 (citations omitted): "In the prophets, especially Jeremiah, the term ['repent'] commonly appears in covenantal contexts and denotes the return of the people to their covenantal relationship with God. The faithless nation is charged to return to the Lord from whom they have strayed. Also of interest is the number of places where the term ['repent'] denotes a return from exile. The association of these two ideas in this one word so [favored] by the prophets suggests that the return from exile consists of the return to covenant faithfulness. Thus when John and Jesus preach repentance they not only issue a call for the nation to turn back to God, but also announce that the time of the restoration has arrived."

[8] The word for Gospel, εὐαγγέλιον, literally means "good news." This may evoke more imagery from Isaiah's New Exodus prophecy: "Get you up to a high mountain, O Zion, herald of good tidings" (Is. 40:9).

Matthew 5, Jesus never calls God "Father," yet within these three chapters He does so seventeen times. This shows us that the "kingdom of God" is also the "Family of God." Not surprisingly, this is where Jesus teaches His followers to pray the "Our Father."

In Matthew 10, Jesus sends out twelve apostles, who are to go only "to the lost sheep of the house of Israel," saying, "The kingdom of heaven is at hand" (Mt. 10:6-7). Here the restoration imagery is clear. Jesus appoints twelve apostles, corresponding to the twelve tribes of Israel, who are to go out to Israelites. Professor Edward Sri explains: "This action alone would have signaled that all the Jewish hopes for a renewed Israel were coming to fulfillment in Jesus' movement."[9]

Later on, Jesus is walking through the grain fields plucking ears of grain to eat. The Pharisees accuse Jesus of violating the Sabbath, because Exodus 34:21 forbids harvesting on the Sabbath.[10] Jesus responds by comparing Himself to David, who ate the consecrated bread of the Temple when he was fleeing Saul:

> Have you not read what David did, when he was hungry, and those who were with him: how he entered the house of God and ate the bread of the Presence, which it was not lawful for him to eat nor for those who were with him, but only for the priests? (Mt. 12:3-4).

Later in the chapter, Jesus again refers to His Davidic pedigree: "[B]ehold, something greater than Solomon is here" (Mt. 12:42).

---

[9] Sri, *Mystery of the Kingdom*, 86.

[10] Deuteronomy 23:25 actually distinguishes between "harvesting" and "plucking grain," but the Pharisees simply prohibited both by their own strict interpretation of the law. See Hahn and Mitch, *Gospel of Matthew*, 36.

Matthew 16 depicts Jesus giving Peter "the keys of the kingdom" (Mt. 16:19). This is undoubtedly a reference to Isaiah 22:22, where Shebna is removed from the office of prime minister of the Davidic kingdom and Eliakim is installed in his place. Isaiah states: "I will place on his shoulder the key of the house of David; he shall open, and none shall shut; and he shall shut, and none shall open" (Is. 22:22). Isaiah's words about "opening" and "shutting" are certainly echoed in the words Jesus tells Peter: "whatever you bind on earth shall be bound in heaven, and whatever you loose on earth shall be loosed in heaven" (Mt. 16:19).[11]

Near the conclusion of the Gospel, we can see further kingdom imagery in Jesus' statement to Caiaphas: "But I tell you, hereafter you will see the Son of man seated at the right hand of Power, and coming on the clouds of heaven" (Mt. 26:64). This is surely a reference to Daniel's prophecy, which foretold that the Son of Man would come to receive the kingdom and give it to the saints (cf. Dan. 7:13-14, 22).

Finally, Jesus' closing words to the apostles at the end of the Gospel signal the restoration of the kingdom. Jesus states that the apostles are to go to "all nations," baptizing them and making them disciples. Jesus is thereby fulfilling God's plan to bring all the nations back to Himself, united with Israel, under the Davidic king.

In this brief survey, we have seen how Jesus understood His ministry in terms of the restoration of the kingdom. Jesus fulfills the hope of Israel, as all twelve tribes are united with the nations under the Davidic king. Hence, Jesus' ministry could be summed up by the petition of the Our Father, recorded in Matthew 6: "Thy kingdom come."

---

[11] The "keys" are also undeniably linked to the "gates" of Hades, as in Revelation 20:1-3.

CHAPTER 7

THE CHURCH:
THE KINGDOM OF GOD
ON EARTH

In looking for the restored kingdom, we should not look for military might, earthly power, wealth, or splendor. These are simply earthly goods. Indeed, to mistake the kingdom of God for these things would constitute nothing less than the fall of Adam, who desired earthly goods over heavenly ones. Rather, the essence of the kingdom is the extension of God's covenant to all men.

How is God's covenant restored? What are men to do if they wish to be saved? This was the question the crowd asked Peter on the feast of Pentecost: "Brethren, what shall we do?" (Acts 2:37). Peter responded to them, saying, "Repent, and be baptized every one of you" (Acts 2:38). Hence, God's covenant relationship is restored to the individual through Baptism.

At the beginning of our study we saw that covenants are established through the swearing of oaths. This holds true as well for the New Covenant established by Christ. The Latin word for oath is *sacramentum*. The pagan writer Pliny recounted how the early Christians gathered to worship on Sunday, "having bound themselves by a solemn oath."[1] Entry into the New Covenant has always been accomplished through the sacraments.

The Sacrament of Baptism initiates us into the New Covenant. This initiation enables us to receive the gift of divine

---

[1] E.O. James, *Sacrifice and Sacrament* (New York: Barnes and Noble, 1962), 14.

sonship. Thus, Baptism involves "rebirth" or "regeneration." Jesus told Nicodemus, "Truly, truly, I say to you, unless one is born of water and the Spirit, he cannot enter the kingdom of God" (Jn. 3:5). Similarly, the Catechism states,

> [B]y Baptism the Christian participates in the grace of Christ. . . . As an "adopted son" he can henceforth call God "Father," in union with the only Son. He receives the life of the Spirit who breathes charity into him and who forms the Church (no. 1997).

Further, just as covenant oath-swearing in the Old Testament involved a verbal promise and ritual enactment, the sacraments are similarly divided up into word and act.

In Baptism, for example, the minister pronounces the words, "I baptize you in the name of the Father, and of the Son, and of the Holy Spirit." While these words are being spoken, a ritual act is performed whereby water is either poured on the new believer or the baptized is immersed. This symbolizes the washing away of sin and the rising to new life in Christ.[2]

Yet, it is in the Eucharist that the hope for the restored kingdom is perfectly realized. Indeed, the Eucharist itself may be understood as Jesus' own *todah* offering. There, Jesus offered Himself through the offering of bread and wine. Further, His death is closely linked to the Last Supper, inasmuch as His death completes the offering He initiated in the Upper Room.

---

[2] See Thomas Aquinas, *Summa Theologiae*, IIIa, q. 66, art. 4. Saint Cyril comments: "What a wonder and a paradox! We have not actually died, we have not really been buried, and we have not, in reality, after having been crucified, risen again. But the imitation is effected in an image (*en eikoni*), salvation in reality (*en aletheia*)." Saint Cyril of Jerusalem, as translated in J.P. Migne, ed., *Patrologia Graeca* (Paris: Garnier and Migne, 1857-1904), XXXIII, 1083B-1084B. See also Jean Danielou, S.J., *The Bible and the Liturgy* (Notre Dame, IN: University of Notre Dame Press, 1956), 44.

The Passover meal was divided into four parts, for which four different cups were served. However, Jesus did not drink the fourth cup at the Last Supper, but rather drank it on the Cross.[3] Once Christ is about to die He drinks sour wine from a hyssop branch and says, "It is finished," and breathes His last (Jn. 19:30). In this, Christ completes the New Passover, which began in the Upper Room.

At That First Eucharist

The fact that Jesus chose the Passover to institute the Eucharist also shows us Jesus' intention to restore the kingdom through it. The Passover was a meal, which celebrated Israel's Exodus out of Egypt. Yet, as time went on, the Passover also became emblematic of the hope for the New Exodus.

> At this festival the people of God remember the merciful immunity grated to the houses marked with the blood of the paschal lamb and the deliverance from Egyptian bondage. At the same time the Passover is *a looking forward to the coming deliverance of* which the deliverance from Egypt is the prototype.[4]

Hence, Rabbinic tradition held that the "Messiah comes in the Passover night."[5]

Thus, the Eucharist—which means "thanksgiving"—is the true Davidic *todah* through which Israel's restoration is accomplished:

> The Last Supper is the thank offering (*todah*) of the One who is risen. . . . [T]he Lord's Supper is the proclamation of the

---

[3] See Hahn, *A Father Who Keeps His Promises*, 224-43.
[4] Jeremias, *The Eucharistic Words of Jesus*, 206 (emphasis added).
[5] *Ibid.*

death of Jesus (1 Cor. 11:26), and at the same time it is praise of God, rejoicing over the salvation God has wrought (cf. Acts 2:46-47).[6]

Moreover, since Christians unite themselves in suffering with Christ, they participate in the same life-giving offering as Jesus. Through drinking the "third" cup in the liturgy, they pledge their own self-offering in union with Him, hoping to also share in His Resurrection (cf. Rom. 6:5).

The Mass, therefore, represents a kind of corporate *todah*, through which we unite ourselves to Christ's act of life-giving love, proclaiming God's deliverance of Him through the Resurrection, as we anticipate our future sharing in it. Hence, Drijvers writes: "All the distinguishing marks of the Jewish ceremony of thanksgiving, and thus also of this group of thanksgiving psalms, we find once again in the Holy Mass."[7] Thus, through the liturgy of the Mass the restoration of the kingdom is celebrated, just as it was hoped for in Jewish liturgical life as reflected in the Psalter.

Just as the Davidic king embodied the experience of Israel, so too does Christ. Indeed, the New Testament frequently explains that Jesus' death was foretold by the prophets by using texts which originally foretold the restoration of Israel.[8] The Resurrection of Jesus' body is therefore the initiation of the restoration of Israel. The Eucharist unites us to this body, completing the restoration.

Moreover, since Christ's offering in the Eucharist is the manifestation in human history of His eternal act of life-giving love to the Father, union with Christ in the Eucharist means union with Christ in the Trinity. This incorporation

---

[6] Gese, *Essays on Biblical Theology*, 134.

[7] Drijvers, *The Psalms, Their Structure and Meaning*, 100.

[8] Indeed, the only "third day" resurrection prophecy pertains to Israel's return from exile (cf. Hos. 6:2).

into the Trinity constitutes nothing less than the attainment of heaven. This was God's purpose all along in restoring man to the covenant of Adam through the Davidic kingdom; man is brought into covenant family union with the Triune God. The restoration, therefore, brings us to the true Zion, the heavenly Jerusalem, of which the earthly one is only a copy. Thus, the Book of Revelation depicts all twelve tribes united with the nations on Mount Zion in heaven (cf. Rev. 7:4-9; 14:1).

At the institution of the Eucharist, Jesus speaks of the New Covenant: "This cup which is poured out for you is the new covenant in my blood" (Lk. 22:20). The term "new covenant" was used only by the prophet Jeremiah, who used it in reference to the restoration of Israel. Thus, after Jeremiah prophesies about the Lord gathering back Israel from being "scattered" to the nations (Jer. 31:10), the prophet goes on to say: "Behold, the days are coming, says the LORD, when I will make a new covenant with the house of Israel and the house of Judah" (Jer. 31:31).

Thus, through the Eucharist Jesus accomplishes the restoration of the kingdom. Jesus tells the apostles, after they have eaten and drunk at the Eucharistic table:

> You are those who have continued with me in my trials; as my Father appointed a kingdom for me, so do I appoint for you that you may eat and drink at my table in my kingdom, and sit on thrones judging the twelve tribes of Israel (Lk. 22:28-30).

The word used here for "appoint" is derived from the Greek word for covenant, διαθήκη. Thus, in the Eucharist Christ "covenants" to His apostles the kingdom. This is because they have partaken of the Eucharist and have been with Him in His suffering. They have united themselves with His eternal self-offering, and are thus the first to participate in the restored kingdom, through which they are united to the Triune God.

The Church is the extension of the kingdom of God on earth, because the Church, through her sacramental ministry, extends God's covenant family relationship to all men.[9] Further, the kingdom of God is present in the Church through the Eucharist, since "where the Eucharist is, there is the King."[10] There the eschatological feast on Mount Zion prophesied in Isaiah 25:6 occurs. Hence, the Church is the restored kingdom, which, in the Eucharist, unites herself with Christ's eternal self-offering, entering into the Trinitarian life. God has become a "sanctuary" and a "dwelling place" for her.[11] Thus, in the Eucharist the Church proclaims "the kingdom, the power, and the glory," because there Christ the King comes to the Church and is present with her.[12]

---

[9] Schönborn explains that Vatican II's description of the Church as "the sacrament of the kingdom" in no way minimizes the fact that the Church is also the kingdom itself: "The *pilgrim* Church is the kingdom that 'buds and grows until the time for the harvest.'" *From Death to Life* (San Francisco: Ignatius Press, 1995), 82, original emphasis.

[10] From Scott Hahn's foreword in Sri, *Mystery of the Kingdom*, 11.

[11] Hence, in Revelation 21:22 John learns that there is no temple in the holy city, because "its temple is the Lord God and the Lamb."

[12] The New Testament term for Christ's second coming, parousia, also means "presence." Hence, Christ's second coming truly is realized in the Eucharistic liturgy. Cardinal Joseph Ratzinger explains: "The Parousia is the highest intensification and fulfillment of the Liturgy. And the Liturgy is Parousia, a Parousia-like event taking place in our midst." *Dogmatic Theology: Eschatology, Death and Eternal Life*, Michael Waldstein, trans. (Washington: Catholic University Press, 1988), 203.

ROMANS 9-11:
GOD'S FATHERLY PLAN
FOR FINDING THE LOST TRIBES

We have seen how the Psalter reflected the hope that *all* Israel—that is, all twelve tribes—would be restored. The southern kingdom of Judah did return from exile in Babylon. However, the northern tribes conquered by Assyria never did. In fact, over time, they were largely assimilated into the Gentile nations. So how could God keep His promise to restore them? That is the issue Saint Paul addresses in Romans 9-11.[1]

Many times Saint Paul is called the "apostle to the Gentiles." However, Paul's mission was also to the Israelites. Jesus told Ananias, who baptized Paul, that he would be His chosen instrument to take His name to "Gentiles and kings and the sons of Israel" (Acts 9:15). Because of this Paul understood that he was not only to carry God's message to the Gentiles, but also to restore *all* the tribes of Israel. This is apparent in Acts 26:7, where Paul tells King Agrippa that he holds fast to the hope "to which our twelve tribes hope to attain." Paul thus embodied the hope reflected in the Psalter—that all the tribes of Israel would be restored, including the ten northern tribes that hadn't been heard from since 722 B.C.

---

[1] The approach taken here to Romans 9-11 takes its cue from the unique insights presented by Scott Hahn in his series of lectures titled, *All Israel Shall Be Saved*, available through Saint Joseph Communications, P.O. Box 1911, Suite 83, Tehachapi, CA 93581 / Phone: out-of-state (800) 526-2151; within California (661) 822-2050.

As we have seen from the Psalter, the hope that all Israel would be saved with the nations is inextricably linked to the hope of the restoration of the Davidic kingdom. This explains why Paul, after establishing his credentials as an apostle, opens his Letter to the Romans by saying that he has been called to preach

> the gospel concerning [God's] Son, who was descended from David according to the flesh and designated Son of God . . . through whom we have received grace and apostleship to bring about the obedience of faith for the sake of his name among all the nations (Rom. 1:3, 5).

Here we see that Jesus' descent from David is linked with the conversion of the nations to God. Through the restoration of Israel, all the nations will be converted (cf. Ps. 68).

And yet it seems that Paul's vision is different from what we would expect. Paul does not say, "After Israel is restored, all nations will be saved." Rather, it seems Paul has it backwards, since he states, "[A] hardening has come upon part of Israel, until the full number of the Gentiles come in, and so all Israel will be saved" (Rom. 11:25-26). Paul appears to believe that it is in the salvation of the Gentiles that Israel is restored.

Context of Divine Sonship

Any way you slice it, this text is difficult to understand. Some interpreters think this means that God withholds the grace of conversion from Israel until the end of time.[2] Others think this means that the "Old Israel" will be replaced with a "New Israel," the Church. In this theory "Israel" is not a name

---

[2] See Merrill Simon, *Jerry Falwell and the Jews* (New York: Jonathon David Publishers, 1984), 47. Jerry Falwell believes that when Christ returns He will establish a sovereign Jewish state. When this occurs the Jews will acknowledge Christ as Lord and convert to Christianity.

for a specific race of people, but instead designates the "people of God." Because of this, a largely Gentile Church can be called "Israel" simply because it represents God's elect.[3] However, both of these views are insufficient since it is clear that Paul refers to the conversion of "ethnic" Israel as well as to the conversion of the Gentiles. So how do we understand this passage?

First, we must consider Romans 9-11 in its original context. These three chapters are not simply an "excursus"—a tangent unrelated to the whole of the Epistle.[4] Indeed, chapters 9-11 stand at the heart of Paul's Letter to the Romans.[5] Therefore, we must begin our examination of Romans 9-11 with a brief look at the chapter that immediately proceeds it.

Romans 8 is primarily concerned with the issue of suffering and its relationship to divine sonship. In 8:17, Paul explains that we are "fellow heirs with Christ, provided we suffer with him."[6] Because of this, when Paul speaks a few verses later about being "conformed to the image" of God's Son, the first-born (Rom. 8:29), we should understand this in terms of suffering in union with Him.[7] As we have seen, divine sonship involves pouring out one's own life in love. In offering up suffering in union with Christ, we share in His act of "life-giving love."

---

[3] Cf. Kim Douhyun, *God, Israel and the Gentiles: Rhetoric and Situation in Romans 9-11* (Ann Arbor, MI: University Microfilms, 1999), 182 *et seq.*

[4] See Elizabeth Johnson, *The Function of Apocalyptic and Wisdom Traditions in Romans 9-11* (Atlanta: Scholars Press, 1989), 122. Johnson explains that a growing number of scholars see Romans 9-11 as an integral part of the Epistle to the Romans and not merely as a postscript or recapitulation.

[5] *Ibid.*

[6] Notice how Paul uses the term "heir," which denotes filial relation.

[7] Thus, Paul says: "What shall separate us from the love of Christ? Shall tribulation, or distress, or persecution, or famine, or nakedness, or peril, or sword? . . . No in all these things we are more than conquerors through him who loved us" (Romans 8:35, 37). In other words, suffering cannot separate us from Christ, but rather, unites us to Him.

This is true not only for individuals, but also for nations, especially Israel, since it is God's first-born son among the nations. Paul goes on to quote a psalm that explains Israel's suffering in exile: "For thy sake we are being killed all the day long; we are regarded as sheep to be slaughtered" (Rom. 8:36; cf. Ps. 44:22). Paul's primary point is that individuals live out their sonship in Christ through suffering. Yet at the same time, Paul's use of the psalm implies that Israel, the first-born among the nations, realized its sonship through suffering as well, through its experience of exile.

Psalmody Could Get Hurt!

Chapter 9 begins with a decided shift in emphasis. Before chapter 9 Paul uses the term "Jew" in Romans. However, in 9-11 Paul only uses the term "Jew" twice. Saint Paul changes his vocabulary and uses the more inclusive term "Israel" or "Israelite" twelve times in three chapters.

Paul begins by saying that he feels great sorrow for his fellow Israelites who have not been saved. After all, he says, to them belong the gifts of

> sonship, the glory, the covenants, the giving of the law, the worship, and the promises; to them belong the patriarchs, and of their race, according to the flesh, is the Christ, who is God over all, blessed for ever (Rom. 9:4-5).

It is noteworthy that the first gift Paul mentions is Israel's sonship, since Romans 8 deals with the topic extensively. Later, we will see the significance of this.

However, even though God gave Israel these promises and gifts, ten-twelfths of Israel remain in exile! They still have not returned! Paul, therefore, addresses the obvious question: "Has God failed His people?" Paul is ready for this question. He replies, "But it is not as though the word of God had failed" (Rom. 9:6). From here Paul begins a carefully constructed argument, demonstrating his masterful understanding of the Old Testament.

Discrimination of a Nation

Because not all of Israel has been saved, we might conclude that God's promise to them has failed. Indeed, in facing the defeat of the Davidic king and the horror of exile, Psalm 89 cries to God: "But now thou hast cast [us] off . . . Thou hast renounced the covenant with thy servant" (vv. 38-39). Paul asserts that this is not the case with a proposition that would have seemed extremely offensive to his own people:

> But it is not as though the word of God had failed. For not all who are descended from Israel belong to Israel, and not all are children of Abraham because they are his descendants; but "Through Isaac shall your descendants be named" (Rom. 9:6-7; cf. Gen. 21:12).

The idea that "not all who are descended from Israel belong to Israel" must have been incredibly controversial. How could Paul discriminate so? Paul's reasoning here is tightly connected with the original Old Testament context.

In Genesis 21:12, God tells Abraham that His covenant promise to bless all nations will be fulfilled by his son Isaac, not Ishmael. Here there is a narrowing of the promise. God identifies the appointed line and sends Ishmael packing, literally. In Genesis 21, we read that Ishmael had been "playing" with Isaac. Yet, the word used here described something more than innocent child's play—Ishmael was "teasing" or "persecuting" his younger brother. Because of this Ishmael was sent away and the "elect" line of Abraham was designated. Paul quotes God's decree to Abraham: "[T]hrough Isaac shall your descendants be named" (Gen. 21:12).

Paul explains: "This means that it is not the children of the flesh who are the children of God, but the children of the promise are reckoned as descendants" (Rom. 9:8). Paul is stressing that biological lineage is not enough to ensure one's status as part of God's people. If that were true, both Isaac and Ishmael would have been recipients of God's covenant oath to bless all nations through Abraham's descendants. Yet, within the chosen line, the line of Abraham, there is further distinction between the "seed of the promise" and the rest. Paul illustrates this by looking at Isaac's sons, Jacob and Esau. Even though God promised to bless all nations through Abraham's divinely appointed heir, not *all* of Isaac's descendants were equal. It is clear that Jacob was chosen over Esau. Paul quotes the prophet Malachi: "Jacob I loved, but Esau I hated" (Rom. 9:13; cf. Mal. 1:2).

Who Shall Be Saved?

At this point we have to wonder whether God is unjust. Does God arbitrarily decide whom He will bless and whom He will condemn? It almost appears as though Paul is arguing for the Calvinist God who predestines some to salvation and others to perdition simply because of His total all-powerful election. At first glance, this kind of "fatalism" seems to be confirmed by what Paul goes on to say.

Saint Paul recalls God's words to Moses after the golden calf incident, "I will have mercy on whom I have mercy, and I will have compassion on whom I have compassion" (Rom. 9:15; cf. Ex. 33:19). He then refers to an image used in the prophets, that of God as potter and His people as clay He forms:

> But who are you, a man, to answer back to God? Will what is molded say to its molder, "Why have you made me thus?" Has the potter no right over the clay, to make out of the same lump one vessel for beauty and another for menial use? (Rom. 9:20-21).

From all of this, it would seem that Paul is describing a heartless God who arbitrarily decrees some as His "elect" and others as the "reprobate," or the damned. Yet, to read these passages this way is to wrench them completely out of context.

First, let us consider the big picture. Paul has just shown in Romans 8 that the true calling of sonship entails the offering up of suffering in love. Yet Ishmael did not offer life-giving love, but rather sought to lord his first-born status over his younger brother, Isaac. Because of this, Ishmael was bypassed for Isaac. Likewise, Esau, Isaac's elder son, was bypassed for Jacob.

Thus Paul is buttressing his argument. Not *all* Israelites are automatically saved because of their ethnic status, just as not *all* the descendants of Abraham and Isaac were children of the promise simply by virtue of their biological descent. But how does God decide who gets the promise? How does He decide which Israelites receive the blessing? Is God acting arbitrarily? To answer these questions, Paul turns to Exodus 33.

The events chronicled in Exodus 33 are extremely significant because they immediately follow the sin of the golden calf. Israel deserves death for breaking the covenant. Yet, Moses pleads with God to spare them, and God does so. The reason is "so that my name may be proclaimed in all the earth" (Rom. 9:17; Ex. 9:16).

At this point Saint Paul brings up the image of the potter and the clay, but not to explain how God can arbitrarily save and condemn. Paul's point is that even though Israel may have deserved to be shaped for destruction, God, as the potter, can shape His "clay" however He pleases. Likewise, if the people repent, God is not forced to destroy them. He can shape them into a "vessel of mercy" (Rom. 9:23).

This interpretation is confirmed by the contexts of the Old Testament passages that Paul cites. He first turns to Isaiah,

"Will what is molded say to its molder, 'Why have you made me thus?'" (Rom. 9:20). This seems to be a combination of Isaiah 29:16 and 45:9. In both places the prophet speaks of the wicked in Israel, who think God does not see the evil they commit. Yet the prophet explains that despite their evil intentions, God has a plan to ultimately save His people. God says, "Will you question me?" (Is. 45:11), not because He has the right to condemn anyone He pleases, but because He has the right to save those who do not deserve mercy—like Israel after the golden calf.

Saint Paul may also have in mind the potter imagery in Jeremiah 18. In this passage Jeremiah speaks to the houses of Israel and Judah. He tells them that God is shaping evil against Israel for its sin, but warns Judah not to become self-righteous. After all, the prophet explains, God is the potter and He can re-shape good for the northern kingdom if they repent, and evil for the southern kingdom if they become wicked:

> Behold, like the clay in the potter's hand, so are you in my hand, O house of Israel. If at any time I declare concerning a nation or a kingdom, that I will pluck it up and break down and destroy it, and if that nation, concerning which I have spoken, turns from its evil, I will repent of the evil that I intended to do to it. And if at any time I declare concerning a nation or a kingdom that I will build and plant it, and if it does evil in my sight, not listening to my voice, then I will repent of the good which I had intended to do to it. . . . Behold, I am shaping evil against you and devising a plan against you. Return, every one from his evil way, and amend your ways and your doings (Jer. 18:6-11).

From this, it is clear that the image of the potter demonstrates God's readiness to show mercy, and does not depict a fatalistic divine decree.

Come Back to Me

So how does this relate to Israel? Saint Paul indicates that Israel deserved exile for its sin, much like it deserved death following the golden calf. In fact, the northern kingdom itself fell back into the sin of golden calf worship before being exiled (2 Kings 17:16-18). For this reason, like the generation of Moses' time, they deserved punishment; they deserved to be exiled. And yet God promised to save them since He is the Potter, who can even reshape an unworthy lump.

Paul now launches into a series of texts that foretell the return of the lost northern tribes. In Hosea, God explains that He will scatter the northern tribes to the nations because of their wickedness. Hence, God refers to them as "Not my people" and "Not pitied" (Hos. 1:6, 9). Nonetheless, God promises that one day He will bring them back and have pity on them (cf. Hos. 1:10; 2:23). When Paul speaks of some of the Israelites who are called from the nations in the context of Hosea 1-2, he is referring to the return of the "lost" tribes of Israel. Speaking now of these lost tribes, Paul takes the prophet (and God) at his word—"And in the very place where it was said to them, 'You are not my people,' they will be called 'sons of the living God'" (Rom. 9:26; cf. Hos. 1:10).

The Few, the Proud, the Remnant

Paul next turns to prophecies from Isaiah. Here he introduces a new concept into the argument: the remnant. Isaiah prophesied that—though the Israelites in his day were as numerous as the stars—after God's punishment, only a "remnant" would be saved (Rom. 9:27; cf. Is. 10:22-23). God would preserve a remnant because if He did not, Israel would be destroyed like Sodom and Gomorrah (Rom. 9:29; cf. Is. 1:9). So, while God scattered the northern tribes, He allowed those in the south to return from captivity. Judah was spared. This is why Isaiah 1:8 speaks of Zion that is "left like a booth in a vineyard, like lodge in a cucumber field." The Jews who dwell in Jerusalem represent the "few survivors" mentioned in Isaiah 1:9.

However, these "survivors" in Jerusalem are not righteous themselves. Thus, the rulers of Israel are called the rulers of Sodom (Is. 1:10)—because once they are judged, no survivors will remain. Israel will be completely decimated, like the people of Sodom. The sacrifices of the Jews in the Temple are detestable to God, since the people have become evil. Their offerings are made in "vain" (Is. 1:13). Both houses of Israel have fallen. Neither one of the houses represents the singular "chosen line." This is what we saw in looking at psalms like Psalm 55. There David explains that even his own fellow Israelites persecute him. Indeed, "no one is righteous" (cf. Ps. 14:3), not the Gentiles, not Israel.

Paul further explains his case by combining two passages in Isaiah. First, he cites Isaiah 28:16, "Behold, I am laying in Zion for a foundation a stone, a tested stone." He ties this together with Isaiah 8:14: "And [the Lord] will become a sanctuary, and a stone of offense, and a rock of stumbling to both houses of Israel, a trap and a snare to the inhabitants of Jerusalem." What unites both these passages is the "stone" laid down by the Lord.

This stone, called the "foundation stone," originally referred to the Temple, which was built upon a huge rock at its foundation. This stone became a stumbling stone to the northern tribes who, upon pledging their allegiance the king of the north, disregarded God's Temple in Jerusalem. They would not worship in the Temple built by the Judahite king. They would not recognize that their rival kingdom had the holy place of the worship of the one true God. So instead, they began worshipping pagan gods at their own high places.

Paul has a keen insight here. Isaiah prophesied that the Lord would become a stone, a "sanctuary" (Is. 8:14), the true

Temple. This is fulfilled by Jesus, who tells the Jews that He is the true Temple (Jn. 2:19-21). In rejecting Jesus the Jews fulfill Isaiah's prophecy, stumbling over the "cornerstone," and acting as the northern kingdom did by rejecting God's true Temple.

Conversely, the Gentiles have been saved because they did not stumble over the "stone." The Jews rejected Christ because He rejected their Temple. Just like the northern tribes who refused to submit to God's true Temple out of nationalistic pride, the Jews rejected Christ because He brought about access to the true Temple in the Heavenly Jerusalem, making the earthly Jerusalem obsolete. Meanwhile, the Gentiles had already been humbled. As a result they did not stumble over the "stone of offense." The law made Israel proud, thinking they received it because of the people's righteousness. However, we have seen that they received the ceremonial law because of their sin at the golden calf, not because of their unimpeachable righteousness.

Wholly Moses

Saint Paul begins Romans 10 by stressing his desire that his own people, Israel, be saved (Rom. 10:1). Particularly, Paul has in mind the Jews, the members of the southern house of Judah, who continue to stumble over the Jerusalem Temple. Paul states that his people have not yet been "enlightened," since they have not recognized Christ, who is the fulfillment of the law (Rom. 10:2-4). He proceeds to show how the law was meant to lead one to life.

First, Paul cites Leviticus 18:5, "You shall therefore keep my statutes and ordinances, by doing which a man shall live" (cf. Rom. 10:5). Earlier, however, we saw that this law was given because of Israel's sin. Indeed, Ezekiel says that this law was "not good" and tells us that even those who obeyed it "could not have life" through it (Ezek. 20:25). Has God contradicted Himself? Did He forget the words that He spoke through Moses in Leviticus? Of course not.

The fact that the law was insufficient was the reason God gave it to Israel. The people of Israel were meant to be humbled by it and recognize their inability to turn from sin on their own. God gave Israel a law to quarantine them from other nations. However, instead of being humbled and acknowledging their weakness, the Israelites took pride in the law and saw it as an end in itself. The law was supposed to help them realize their weakness and cause them to call out to God for help. In this sense the law would have led to life. The law was supposed to give way to a trusting faith, through which Israel would place their hope in God rather than their own ability.

To illustrate all of this Paul harkens back to Moses' address to Israel in Deuteronomy. There Moses tries to teach this lesson to Israel. Moses enjoins the people to obey the law, saying:

> For this commandment which I command you this day is not too hard for you, neither is it far off. It is not in heaven, that you should say, "Who will go up for us to heaven, and bring it to us, that we may hear it and do it?" Neither is it beyond the sea, that you should say, "Who will go over the sea for us, and bring it to us, that we may hear it and do it?" But the word is very near you; it is in your mouth and in your heart, so that you can do it (Deut. 30:11-14).

Moses is trying to teach the people that the ability to keep the law is not far from them—all they have to do is ask for God's help. In the preceding chapter, Moses alludes to this truth. He tells the people that they still do not have a mind to understand, eyes to see, or ears to hear, because the Lord has not given them these things (Deut. 29:4). Why not? Because the people are too proud to ask God for help. They think they can keep the law on their own.

In fact, from the beginning of Deuteronomy Moses emphasizes this point, telling the people what they need to do to be saved: "Circumcise therefore the foreskin of your heart" (Deut. 10:16). When the people heard this, they should have realized that they could not cure themselves, since no one can circumcise his own heart. Yet, the people do not acknowledge their insufficiency. In Deuteronomy 30, Moses foresees Israel's sin and the exile that would follow. He explains that only after Israel is humbled by the exile will they then turn to God. On that day, Moses explains, "the LORD your God will circumcise your heart" (Deut. 30:6). The Lord will do it, because the people cannot.

This is the larger context evoked by Paul, who explains that the law is now fulfilled in Christ:

> But what does it say? The word is near you on your lips and in your heart (that is, the word of faith which we preach); because, if you confess with your lips that Jesus is Lord and believe in your heart that God raised him from the dead, you will be saved. . . . For there is no distinction between Jew and Greek (Rom. 10:8-9, 12; cf. Deut. 30:14).

Grace is only a prayer away. The ability to keep the law is now a reality, because faith in Christ fulfills the law by giving us the power to keep it. Salvation is not based on the observance of the ceremonial works of the law, as the Jews in Paul's day held. Notice that in Romans 10:12 Paul reverts to the term "Jew," whereas throughout 9-11 he uses the broader term "Israelite." This is because it is specifically the Jews who still cling to the ceremonial Temple code in Jerusalem.

Only in exile does Israel come to see that God does not desire the blood of animals, but "[t]he sacrifice acceptable to God is a broken spirit; a broken and contrite heart, O God, thou wilt not despise" (Ps. 51:17). The exile is meant to be, above all else, a lesson in redemptive suffering.

The Suffering Servant

Indeed, once Israel is humbled and returns to the Lord, it will seek to fulfill its first calling—to convert the nations. Because of this Saint Paul cites several passages that speak of the mission to bring all peoples back to the Lord. He first cites Joel, who prophesied that a remnant from all nations will be saved in Zion when God restores His people (cf. Joel 3:1-2). Paul draws from Joel 2:32, which states: "And it shall come to pass that all who call upon the name of the LORD shall be delivered."

At this point, Paul asks, Who will go out to Israel and the nations and tell them God's appointed time has come? Paul turns to Isaiah's prophecy concerning the suffering servant: "[W]ho has believed what he has heard from us?" (Rom. 10:16; cf. Is. 53:1). The suffering servant brings about the redemption of the peoples through being rejected and afflicted. The Lord explains in Isaiah 52:10 that He will redeem His people and bring salvation to the ends of the earth: "The LORD has bared his holy arm before the eyes of all the nations" (Is. 52:10). Yet, the Lord reveals Himself to the peoples, not by military strength but through His suffering servant:

> And to whom has the arm of the LORD been revealed? For he grew up before him like a young plant, and like a root out of dry ground; he had no form or comeliness that we should look at him, and no beauty that we should desire him. He was despised and rejected by men. . . . But he was wounded for our transgressions, he was bruised for our iniquities . . . with his stripes we are healed. . . . when he makes himself an offering for sin, he shall see his offspring (Is. 53:1-3, 5, 10).

Through the self-offering and life-giving love of the servant, the world is saved. Of course, this is fulfilled ultimately in Christ. Yet, Paul may have understood himself in terms of a suffering servant as well.

Paul has already explained what it means to be conformed to the image of Christ, the true Suffering Servant: "[We are] fellow heirs with Christ, provided we suffer with him" (Rom. 8:17). Instead of separating us from Christ, suffering actually unites us to Him. That is why Paul explains that through tribulation, distress, persecution, famine, nakedness, peril, and the sword we are made "more than conquerors" (Rom. 8:35, 37).

Curses!!!

It is also important to note, though, that Saint Paul's list of possible afflictions is a summary of the covenant curses Moses warned Israel would trigger if they failed to keep the law (cf. Lev. 26; Deut. 28). Paul is saying that just as Christ was accursed and hung on a cross, so too Christians may participate in His suffering, redemptively bearing the curses of the law. Only through being afflicted and accursed did the Suffering Servant, Christ, bring salvation to the world. Likewise, those who are His messengers may experience similar persecution, and thus be able to offer up their suffering for those they seek to evangelize.

This is what Paul means in Romans 9:3 when he wishes he could be "accursed" for the salvation of his fellow Israelites. Indeed, it would seem Paul got his wish. Paul enumerates his own sufferings in 2 Corinthians 11:23-28:

> Are they servants of Christ? I am a better one—I am talking like a madman—with far greater labors, far more imprisonments, with countless beatings, and often near death. Five times I have received at the hands of the Jews the forty lashes less one. Three times I have been beaten with rods; once I was stoned. Three times I have been shipwrecked; a night and a day I have been adrift at sea; on frequent journeys, in danger from rivers, danger from robbers, danger from my own people, danger from Gentiles, danger in the city, danger in the wilderness, danger at sea, danger from false brethren; in

toil and hardship, through many a sleepless night, in hunger and thirst, often without food, in cold and exposure. And, apart from other things, there is the daily pressure upon me of my anxiety for all the churches.

Paul is truly a "suffering servant" of Christ. Through his affliction he receives the power to evangelize.

Underscoring God's desire to save all nations, Paul refers to Psalm 19:4, which speaks of God's Word going out to "the ends of the world." But Paul goes on to explain how the salvation of the Gentiles will bring about the restoration of Israel. Paul is coming to the climax of his argument.

Zealous and Jealous

Paul shows how the jealousy of the Israelites will aid in their salvation. Quoting Deuteronomy 32:21, he shows how the salvation of the Gentiles will lead Israel back to God. Jealousy is a major motif in Israel's history. Israel continually sins because of its to desire to "be like all the nations" (1 Sam. 8:5; cf. Ezek. 20:32; 2 Kings 17:11; 2 Chron. 13:9). As we have seen, God had to give them the law precisely for this reason. Nevertheless, God is a loving Father. He knows how to use "child psychology" to teach us what we need. Because of this God's answer to the Israelites is simple, "You want to be like the nations? Okay. I will teach them My ways and they will return to Me, and then you can follow their example all you want!"

Paul emphasizes that God has not forgotten about the Israelites. "I ask, then, has God rejected his people? By no means! I myself am an Israelite, a descendant of Abraham, a member of the tribe of Benjamin" (Rom. 11:1). Paul is acutely aware of the tribal distinctions. He is a Jew, because he is a member of the tribe of Benjamin, which joined itself to the southern kingdom of Judah. Yet, Paul is aware that there are other *Israelites*, non-Jews, still in exile. God has not forgotten them, even though Paul does not know where they are.

Paul recalls God's words to Elijah, when God reassured him that a righteous remnant from Israel had been preserved, though they seemed nowhere to be found (cf. 2 Kings 19). In fact, Elijah was sent to the same *northern* tribes lost in exile.

This remnant Paul speaks about exists only by God's grace (Rom. 11:5-6). They have not earned remnant status by anything they have done on their own. Only through God's grace have they been preserved.

Paul explains that God allowed Israel to be hardened and sent into exile, quoting Isaiah, "God gave them a spirit of stupor, eyes that should not see and ears that should not hear" (Rom. 11:8; cf. Is. 29:10). Israel rejected its mission to go out to the nations and convert them, so God allowed them to fall deep into sin so that they would eventually be exiled. Does this mean they have been forgotten by God? Paul explains:

> So I ask, have they stumbled so as to fall? By no means! But through their trespass salvation has come to the Gentiles, so as to make Israel jealous. Now if their trespass means riches for the world, and if their failure means riches for the Gentiles, how much more will their full inclusion mean! (Rom. 11:11-12).

In other words, because Israel continued to sin, especially by desiring to be like the Gentiles, the Gentiles themselves would have to be converted for Israel to be saved.

At this point in the epistle, Paul stops and warns the Gentiles not to be smug in their own conversion. It would be easy for the Gentiles to assume that they were better than Israel, since they heard the Gospel when Israel was hardened. Paul uses the analogy of a tree. Israel is the root. Those Israelites who fail to hear the Lord are likened to branches cut off. Conversely, Gentiles who hear the Gospel are compared to wild branches taken from another tree, grafted on to the holy root. Nonetheless, Paul warns, if God can cut off the original branches and graft on wild branches, it is even easier for him to remove the wild ones and restore the original branches.

Saving the Blessed for Last

Now Paul reaches the climax of his argument.

> I want you to understand this mystery, brethren: a hardening has come upon part of Israel, until the full number of Gentiles come in, and so all Israel will be saved (Rom. 11:25-26).

God originally intended Israel to go out to the nations and convert them, but Israel refused. Instead, they wanted to be like other nations. However, as Paul says later, "For the gifts and the call of God are irrevocable" (Rom. 11:29). So Israel has no choice—one way or another they are going to go out to the nations and bring them back.

Instead of being sent as missionaries to the nations, Israel is sent out as captives. They intermarry and become assimilated into the nations. As Hosea prophesied, they become "Not my people" (Hos. 1:9). Still, God promises to restore the kingdom, *all twelve tribes*, and the nations. He does not promise that He will save every single Israelite, but that a remnant will be spared from *all* of Israel, from all the tribes of Israel.

Since Israel has assimilated with the nations, though, God can only save Israel by saving the nations. By saving the Gentiles, then, *all* Israel will be saved. Paul is going to the sons of Israel and the Gentiles because after the exile they are one and the same. Thus, God's plan for Israel is fulfilled: By being sent out to the nations, Israel brings them back when they are restored. Paul summarizes:

Just as you were once disobedient to God but now have received mercy because of their disobedience, so they have now been disobedient in order that by the mercy shown to you they also may receive mercy (Rom. 11:30-31).

How does this fit into a book about the Psalms? The Book of Psalms looks forward to the restoration of Israel. Paul shows how this occurs through his ministry to the Gentiles. Israel has been assimilated into the nations. Like sugar dissolved into tea, God can't bring out Israel without saving the nations with them. This was His plan from the beginning, to use Israel as an instrument to save all peoples, just as He promised Abraham: "Through your descendants all nations shall be blessed" (Gen. 22:18). Israel's exile is nothing less than suffering. Through the affliction of the exile, the nations are saved.

But more than that, it looks forward to the fulfillment of the Father's plan, His *oikonomia*, in which His children learn self-giving love and enter into the life of the Trinity. Paul shows us how the suffering of the exile fits into this plan. If Israel is to fulfill its calling to be God's son, it must look to the example of David. David taught Israel what divine sonship meant. He offered his life in love through suffering—life-giving love—through the *todah*. This is an image of the true Son of God, Jesus, who from all eternity pours His life back to the Father through the Spirit in the life-giving love of the Trinity. His death on the Cross is the human manifestation of that total love which holds nothing back. His death shows us what self-giving love looks like; it is suffering.

Through the exile, the righteous remnant of Israel learns to offer its life in love, through suffering. In this, Israel is conformed to the image of the first-born Son, Christ, who gives His life in love. The righteous remnant of Israel, then, fulfills its calling to divine sonship by learning to offer up in love its suffering in exile. Through this God's people enter into the very life of God, so that He truly becomes their "dwelling place" (Ps. 90:1).

THE STRUCTURE OF
THE BOOK OF PSALMS

BOOK I
Individual psalms of David. David is presented as the exemplary wise man who offers his life in sacrifice through the *Todah* offering.

> Ps. 1-2   Introduction to the Psalter
> Ps. 3-41 Prayers of David
> Ps. 37-41 David at the end of his life

BOOKS II-III
Community oriented. Presents the rise and fall of the Davidic kingdom, as Israel applies David's songs of suffering to its own corporate experience.
Arrangement with David at the center.

Ps. 42-49 Korah psalms

Ps. 50   Asaph psalm
- predicts the "day of trouble" recounted in the last Asaph psalm (Ps. 83).

Ps. 51-72 Davidic psalms
- David is at the center of this collection, high-lighting his central role.
- The glory and splendor of Solomon's reign, explained in Psalm 72, was fleeting. Psalm 73 shows the harsh reality of an unfulfilled promise.

Ps. 73-83 Asaph psalms

Ps. 84-88 Korah psalms
- very similar to the first Korah collection:

42-43	84	Psalms of longing for Yahweh's dwelling place
44	85	National lament
46,48	87	"Song of Zion"

Ps. 89   Fall of the Davidic dynasty and Israel sent into exile.

BOOK IV
Mosaic/Exodus themes are dominant. Israel in exile looks forward to the New Exodus promised by the prophets.

>   Ps. 90-100   Mosaic/Exodus psalms
>   - The hope for a New Exodus.
>
>   Ps. 104-06   Summary of salvation history.
>   - All salvation history is leading up to the
>   restoration of Israel.

BOOK V
Restoration from exile, climaxing with a high concentration of songs of praise.

>   Ps. 107-18   The kingdom is restored.
>   - The Davidic king reappears in 108 and
>   offers *Todah* as he is persecuted in 109.

107-10	*Davidic psalms*
111-18	*praise psalms*
120-34	*Ascent psalms*
135-36	*praise psalms*
138-45	*Davidic psalms*
146-50	*praise psalms*

>   - In 110 the Messiah-King triumphs. He is
>   like Melchizedek who offered bread and wine.
>   His people offer themselves with him on
>   God's holy mountain.
>   - The hallel psalms (111-13; 114-18)
>   are sung in celebration of the restoration.
>
>   Ps. 119   Wisdom/Torah psalm
>   - This wisdom psalm stands at the center of
>   Book V, showing that keeping God's law and
>   teaching it to the nations is the central result
>   and purpose of the restoration (cf. Is. 2:3).
>
>   Ps. 120-36   Exile to Praise
>   - The Ascent psalms (120-34) move from
>   exile to restoration and are capped with praise
>   psalms, like the hallel psalms.
>
>   Ps. 137-50   Conclusion
>   - A final movement from exile, through
>   Davidic psalms, to jubilant climax.

RECOMMENDED READING

Mitchell, David. C., *The Message of the Psalter:
An Eschatological Programme in the Book of Psalms*
(Sheffield, England: Sheffield Press, 1993).

McNeil, Brian, *Christ in the Psalms*
(New York: Paulist Press, 1980).

McCann, J. Clinton, ed., *The Shape and Shaping of the Psalter*
(Sheffield, England: Sheffield Press, 1993).

Loffink, Norbert and Erich Zenger, *The God of Israel and the
Nations: Studies in Isaiah and the Psalms* (Collegeville, MN:
Liturgical Press, 2000).

St. Gregory of Nyssa, *Commentary on the Inscriptions of
the Psalms* (Brookline, MA: Hellenic College Press, 1994).

Ryan, Thomas F., *Thomas Aquinas as Reader of the Psalms*
(Notre Dame, IN: University of Notre Dame Press, 2000).

Jaki, Stanley, *Praying the Psalms: A Commentary*
(Grand Rapids, MI: Eerdmans Publishing Co., 2001).

Guthrie, Harvey, *Theology As Thanksgiving:
From Israel's Psalms to the Church's Eucharist*
(New York: Seabury Press, 1981).

Christian Prayer: The Liturgy of the Hours (Boston, MA:
Daughters of St. Paul, 1976), or other editions of the
Liturgy of the Hours.

*Most of the above may be purchased by calling Benedictus
Books toll-free at (888) 316-2640, or by visiting your local
Catholic bookstore. Readers are also encouraged to subscribe to
Magnificat (800-317-6689), a monthly publication that helps
lay people to pray the Psalms.*

BIBLIOGRAPHY

Books

Aquinas, Thomas, *Summa Theologiae*.

Balthasar, Hans urs Von, *Credo: Meditations on the Apostles' Creed* (New York: Crossroad Publishing, 1990).

Bandstra, Barry, *Reading the Old Testament: An Introduction to the Hebrew Bible* (Belmont, CA: Wadsworth Publishing Company, 1995).

Blaine, Charette, *Restoring Presence: The Spirit in Matthew's Gospel* (Sheffield, England: Sheffield Academic Press, 2000).

Boadt, Lawrence, *Reading the Old Testament: An Introduction* (New York: Paulist Press, 1985).

Broyles, Craig, *New International Biblical Commentary: Psalms* (Peabody, MA: Hendrickson Publishers, 1999).

Campbell, J. McLeod, *The Nature of the Atonement* (Edinburgh: Handsel Press, 1996).

Charlesworth, James, ed., *The Old Testament Pseudepigrapha* (New York: Doubleday, 1998).

Cole, Robert, *The Shape and Message of Book III (Psalms 73-89)* (Sheffield, England: Sheffield Academic Press, 2000).

Congar, Yves, *Tradition and Traditions* (San Diego, CA: Basilica Press, 1966).

Crane, Frank, ed., *The Bible and the Forgotten Books of Eden* (Newfoundland: World Bible Publishers, 1927).

Crawley, Earnest, *Oath, Curse, and Blessing* (London: Watts & Co., 1934).

Creach, Jerome F.D., *Yahweh As Refuge and the Editing of the Hebrew Psalter* (Sheffield, England: Sheffield Press, 1996).

Cross, F.M., "The Themes of the Book of Kings and the Structure of the Deuteronomistic History," *Reconsidering Israel and Judah: Recent Studies on the Deuteronomistic*

History, Gary Knoppers and J. Gordon McConville, eds. (Winona Lake, IN: Eisenbrauns, 2000).

Danielou, S.J., Jean, *The Bible and the Liturgy* (Notre Dame, IN: University of Notre Dame Press, 1956).

Danielou, S.J., Jean, *From Shadows to Reality*, Wulstan Hibberd, trans. (Westminster, MD: The Newman Press, 1960).

De Margerie, Bertrand, *The Christian Trinity in History* (Petersham, MA: St. Bede's Publications, 1982).

Drijvers, Pius, *The Psalms: Their Structure and Meaning* (New York: Herder and Herder, 1965).

Driver, S.R., *An Introduction to the Literature of the Old Testament* (New York: Scribner's Press, 1891).

Eaton, John H., *Kingship and the Psalms* (Naperville, IL: Alec R. Allenson, 1976).

Foss, Martin, *Death, Sacrifice, and Tragedy* (Lincoln, NE: University of Nebraska Press, 1966).

Freyne, Sean, *Galilee, Jesus and the Gospels: Literary Approaches and Historical Investigations* (Philadelphia: Fortress Press, 1988).

Friedman, Richard, *Who Wrote the Bible?* (New York: Summit Books, 1989).

Gage, Warren Austin, *The Gospel of Genesis* (Winona Lake, IN: Carpenter Books, 1984).

Gese, Hartmut, *Essays on Biblical Theology* (Minneapolis: Augsburg Publishing House, 1981).

Gordon, Robert P., *I & II Samuel: A Commentary* (Grand Rapids, MI: Zondervan Publishing House, 1986).

Grottanelli, Cristiano, *Kings and Prophets: Monarchic Power, Inspired Leadership, and Sacred Text in Biblical Narrative* (New York: Oxford University Press, 1999).

Gunkel, Hermann, *The Psalms: A Form Critical Introduction* (Philadelphia: Fortress Press, 1967).

Guthrie, Harvey, *Theology As Thanksgiving: From Israel's Psalms to the Church's Eucharist* (New York: Seabury Press, 1981).

Hahn, Scott, *A Father Who Keeps His Promises* (Ann Arbor, MI: Servant Publications, 1998).

Hahn, Scott, *Kinship by Covenant: A Biblical Theological Study of Covenant Types and Texts in the Old and New Testaments* (Ann Arbor, MI: University Microfilms, 1995).

Hahn, Scott, *The Lamb's Supper* (New York: Doubleday, 1999).

Hahn, Scott, "Prima Scriptura," *The Church and the Universal Catechism: Proceedings from the Fifteenth Convention of the Fellowship of Catholic Scholars*, Rev. Anthony Mastroeni, ed. (Steubenville, OH: Franciscan University Press, 1992).

Hahn, Scott, "The Mystery of the Family of God," *Catholic For A Reason*, Scott Hahn and Leon J. Suprenant, Jr., eds. (Steubenville, OH: Emmaus Road Publishing, 1998).

Halpern, Ben, "Zion in Modern Literature: II. Hebrew Prose," *Zion in Jewish Literature*, Abraham S. Halkin, ed. (Lenham, MI: University Press of America, 1988).

Hess, Richard and Gordon Wenham, *Zion: City of Our God* (Grand Rapids, MI: William B. Eerdmans Publishing, 1990).

Horsley, Richard, *Archaeology, History and Society in Galilee* (Valley Forge, PA: Trinity Press International, 1996).

Horsley, Richard, *Jesus and the Spiral of Violence: Popular Resistance in Roman Palestine* (San Francisco: Harper & Row Publishers, 1987).

Hugenberger, Gordon, *Marriage As a Covenant* (Grand Rapids, MI: Baker Books, 1994).

James, E.O., *Sacrifice and Sacrament* (New York: Barnes and Noble, 1962).

Jeremias, Joachim, *The Eucharistic Words of Jesus* (London: SCM Press, 1960).

Josephus, *The Works of Josephus: New Updated Edition,*
William Whiston, trans. (Peabody, MA: Hendrickson
Publishers, 1987).

Kaiser, Walter, *The Messiah in the Old Testament*
(Grand Rapids, MI: Zondervan Publishing House, 1995).

Kalluveettil, Paul, *Declaration and Covenant*
(Rome: Biblical Institute Press, 1982).

Keck, Leander, *et al.*, eds., *The New Interpreter's Bible*
(Nashville, TN: Abingdon Press, 1994).

Kline, Meredith, *Images of the Spirit*
(Eugene, OR: Wipf and Stock Publishers, 1998).

Kline, Meredith, *Kingdom Prologue*
(South Hampton, MA: M.G. Kline, 1993).

Kline, Meredith, *Treaty of the Great King* (Grand Rapids, MI:
William B. Eerdmans Publishing, 1963).

Kraus, Hans-Joachim, *Theology of the Psalms*
(Minneapolis: Augsburg Publishing House, 1986).

Kugel, James L., *The Bible As It Was*
(Cambridge, MA: Belknap Press, 1997).

Kuschel, Karl-Josef, *Abraham: Sign of Hope for Jews,*
Christians and Muslims (New York: Continuum, 1995).

Laato, Antti, *A Star Is Rising: The Historical Development of*
the Old Testament Royal Ideology and the Rise of the Jewish
Messianic Expectations (Atlanta: Scholars Press, 1997).

Leithart, Peter J., *The Kingdom and the Power* (Phillipsburg,
NJ: Presbyterian & Reformed Publishing, 1993).

Levenson, John D., *Sinai and Zion*
(New York: Harper & Row, 1985).

Mays, James Luther, *Psalms* (Louisville, KY: John Knox Press,
1994).

McCann, J. Clinton, ed., *The Shape and Shaping of the Psalter*
(Sheffield, England: Sheffield Academic Press, 1993).

McCann, J. Clinton, *Yahweh as Refuge* (Sheffield, England:
Sheffield Press, 1993).

McCarthy, D.J., *Old Testament Covenant: A Survey of Current Opinions* (Richmond, VA: John Knox Press, 1972).

McCarthy, D.J., *Treaty and Covenant* (Rome: Pontifical Biblical Institute, 1963).

McGill, Arthur C., *Suffering: A Test of Theological Method* (Philadelphia: The Westminster Press, 1982).

Mettinger, T., *King and Messiah: The Civil and Sacral Legitimation of the Israelite Kings* (Lund, Sweden: CWK Gleerup, 1976).

Meyer, Ben, *Five Speeches That Changed The World* (Collegeville, MN: The Liturgical Press, 1994).

Milgrom, Jacob, *The JPS Torah Commentary: Numbers* (New York: The Jewish Publication Society, 1989).

Mitchell, David C., *The Message of the Psalter* (Sheffield, England: Sheffield Press, 1997).

Murphy, Rowland and Elizabeth Huwiler, *Proverbs, Ecclesiastes, Song of Songs* (Peabody, MA: Hendrickson Publishers, 1999).

Newman, Cardinal John Henry, *An Essay on the Development of Christian Doctrine* (Westminster, England: Christian Classics, 1968).

Oppenheimer, Aharon, *The 'Am Ha-Aretz*, I.H. Levine, trans. (Leiden, Sweden: Brill, 1977).

Paczkowski, Mieczyslaw, "The Sacrifice of Isaac in Early Patristic Exegesis," in *The Sacrifice of Isaac in the Three Monotheistic Religions*, Frederic Manns, ed. (Jerusalem: Franciscan Printing Press, 1995).

Pedersen, Johannes, *Israel: Its Life and Culture* (London: Oxford University Press, 1959).

Perdue, Leo, *Wisdom & Creation* (Nashville, TN: Abingdon Press, 1994).

Ratzinger, Cardinal Joseph, *Principles of Catholic Theology: Building Stones for a Fundamental Theology* (San Francisco: Ignatius Press, 1987).

Ratzinger, Cardinal Joseph, *Dogmatic Theology: Eschatology* (Washington: Catholic University Press, 1988).

Ratzinger, Cardinal Joseph, *The Spirit of the Liturgy* (San Francisco: Ignatius Press, 2000).

Rendsburg, Gary A., *Linguistic Evidence for the Northern Origin of Selected Psalms* (Atlanta: Scholars Press, 1990).

Sanders, James A., *The Dead Sea Psalms Scroll* (Ithaca, NY: Cornell University Press, 1967).

Schaper, Joachim, *Eschatology in the Greek Psalter* (Tübingen, Germany: J.C.B. Mohr, 1995).

Scheeben, Matthias, *The Mysteries of Christianity* (St. Louis: B. Herder Book Co., 1946).

Schönborn, Christoph, *From Death to Life* (San Francisco: Ignatius Press, 1995).

Schönborn, Cardinal Christoph, *Loving The Church: Spiritual Exercises Preached in the Presence of Pope John Paul II* (San Francisco: Ignatius Press, 1998).

Shanks, Hershel, *Frank Moore Cross: Conversations with a Bible Scholar* (Washington: Biblical Archaeology Society, 1994).

Sheppard, Gerald, *Wisdom As a Hermeneutical Construct* (New York: Walter de Gruyter, 1980).

Sri, Edward P., *Mystery of the Kingdom* (Steubenville, OH: Emmaus Road Publishing, 1999).

Stuhlmacher, Peter, *Reconciliation, Law & Righteousness: Essays In Biblical Theology* (Philadelphia: Fortress Press, 1986).

Watts, Rikki E., *Isaiah's New Exodus and Mark* (Tübingen: J.C.B. Mohr, 1997).

Wilson, Gerald, *The Editing of the Hebrew Psalter* (Chico, CA: Scholars Press, 1985).

Wright, Chris, *Knowing Jesus Through the Old Testament* (London: Marshall, 1992).

Wright, G. Ernest and Reginald Fuller, *The Book of the Acts of God* (New York: Doubleday, 1957).

Wright, N.T., *Jesus and the Victory of God*
(Minneapolis: Fortress Press, 1996).

Wright, N.T., *The New Testament and the People of God*
(Minneapolis: Fortress Press, 1992).

Articles

Alden, R.L., "Chiastic Psalms (III): A Study in the Mechanics
of Semitic Poetry in Psalms 101-50," *Journal of Evangelical
Theological Studies*, 21 (1978): 199-210.

Brueggemann, Walter and Patrick Miller, "Psalm 73 as a
Canonical Marker," *Journal for the Study of the Old
Testament*, 72 (1996): 48-52.

Guilding, Aileen, "Some Obscured Rubrics and Lectionary
Allusions in the Psalter," *Journal of Theological Studies*,
3 (1952): 41-55.

Hahn, Scott, "The Hunt for the Fourth Cup," *This Rock*, 2
(1991): 7-12.

Harris, Scott, "Proverbs 1:8-19, 20-23 As 'Introduction,'"
Revue Biblique, 107-2 (2000): 211-12.

King, E.G., "The Influence of the Triennial Cycle upon the
Psalter," *Journal of Theological Studies*, 5 (1903): 203-13.

Mays, James, "The Place of the Torah-Psalms in the Psalter,"
Journal of Biblical Literature, 106 (1987): 11.

Miller, P.D., "Psalm 127—The House That Yahweh Builds,"
Journal for the Study of the Old Testament, 22 (1982):
119-32.

Neubauer, A., "Where are the Ten Tribes?" *Jewish Quarterly
Review*, 1 (1889): 14-28.

Quinn, John M., "Triune Self-Giving: One Key to the
Problem of Suffering," *The Thomist*, 44 (1980): 196.

Ratzinger, Cardinal Joseph, "Crisis in Catechesis,"
Canadian Catholic Review, 7 (1983): 178.

Weinfeld, M., "The Loyalty Oath in the Ancient Near East,"
Ugarit-Furschungen, 8 (1976): 379-414.

Wilson, Gerald, "Evidence of Editorial Divisions in the Hebrew Psalter," *Vetus Testamentum*, 3 (1984): 336-52.

Wilson, Gerald, "The Qumran Psalms Scroll (11QPsa) and the Canonical Psalter: Comparison of Editorial Shaping," *Catholic Biblical Quarterly*, 59 (July 1997): 453-54.

Wilson, G.H., "The Use of Royal Psalms at the 'Seams' of the Hebrew Psalter," *Journal for the Study of the Old Testament*, 35 (1986): 85.

EVERYBODY YOU'D EXPECT TO ENDORSE THIS BOOK HELPED TO WRITE IT.

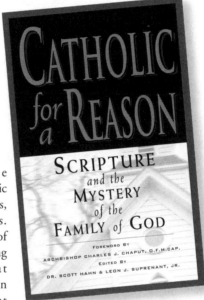

Just imagine today's top Catholic authors, apologists, and theologians. Now imagine 12 of them collaborating on a book that answers common questions about and challenges to the teachings and doctrines of the Catholic Church. Imagine no more, it's a reality. (How's that for an endorsement?)

Catholic for a Reason, edited by Dr. Scott Hahn and Leon J. Suprenant, with the foreword by Archbishop Charles J. Chaput (yes, we're name-dropping), will help Catholics and non-Catholics alike develop a better understanding of the Church. Each chapter goes to the heart of its topic,

presenting the teachings of the Church in a clear, concise and insightful way. The teachings on Mary, the Eucharist, Baptism, and Purgatory are explained in light of the relationship of God the Father to us.

Catholic for a Reason, published by Emmaus Road Publishing, is bound to become an apologetics classic. Call (800) 398-5470 to order your copy today. Retail price $15.95 + $3.00 s/h.

EMMAUS ROAD PUBLISHING

Emmaus Road Publishing
827 North Fourth Street, Steubenville, OH 43952
(800) 398-5470 • Fax: (740) 283-4011
www.emmausroad.org